ARTISTS OF THE NATIONAL LIBRARY OF AUSTRALIA

WOLFGANG SIEVERS

With an essay by Helen Ennis

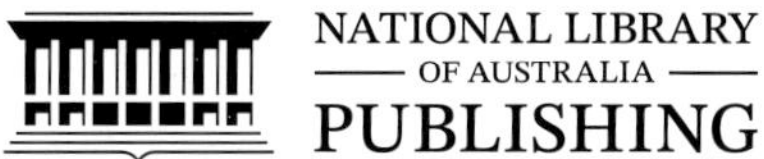

Published by National Library of Australia Publishing
Canberra ACT 2600

ISBN: 9781922507846

The National Library of Australia acknowledges Australia's First Nations Peoples—the First Australians—as the Traditional Owners and Custodians of this land and gives respect to the Elders—past and present—and through them to all Australian Aboriginal and Torres Strait Islander people.

Publisher: Lauren Smith
Managing editors: Amelia Hartney and Rosalind Clarke
Designer: Stan Lamond
Image coordinator: Madeleine Warburton

Printed in China by Asia Pacific Offset on FSC®-certified paper.

Find out more about NLA Publishing at nla.gov.au/national-library-publishing.
A catalogue record for this book is available from the National Library of Australia.

Foreword

The National Library of Australia prides itself on caring for the documentary history of Australia. Our diverse collections of books, magazines, newspapers, manuscripts and pictures provide a rich vein to explore Australian history and culture. Of all the different media collected, photographs are perhaps one of the most powerful and evocative types of material held by the Library. Images of people, streetscapes, buildings, landscapes, working life and leisure invite us to remember what life has been like for all kinds of Australians since the 1850s.

Some of our photographic collections are particularly remarkable for their breadth of content and quality. This book celebrates the Sievers Collection, which is one of the largest photographic archives held by the National Library of Australia. Consisting of over 19,000 prints and 52,000 negatives, the collection documents the work of Wolfgang Georg Sievers. The Library began acquiring Sievers' material in 1996. In 2002, we agreed with Sievers that the Library would become the repository for his entire photographic archive, ensuring that this significant collection would be preserved and made available to the Australian public. In 2003, Sievers, who described himself as 'fiercely Australian but also fiercely European' was made an Officer of the Order of Australia.

This collection is an invaluable resource. Aesthetically stunning and historically significant, these photos provide a clear-sighted vision of how Australia transformed itself after the Second World War. This visual archive helps us understand how Australia has become the country it is.

Dr Guy Hansen
Director, Exhibitions

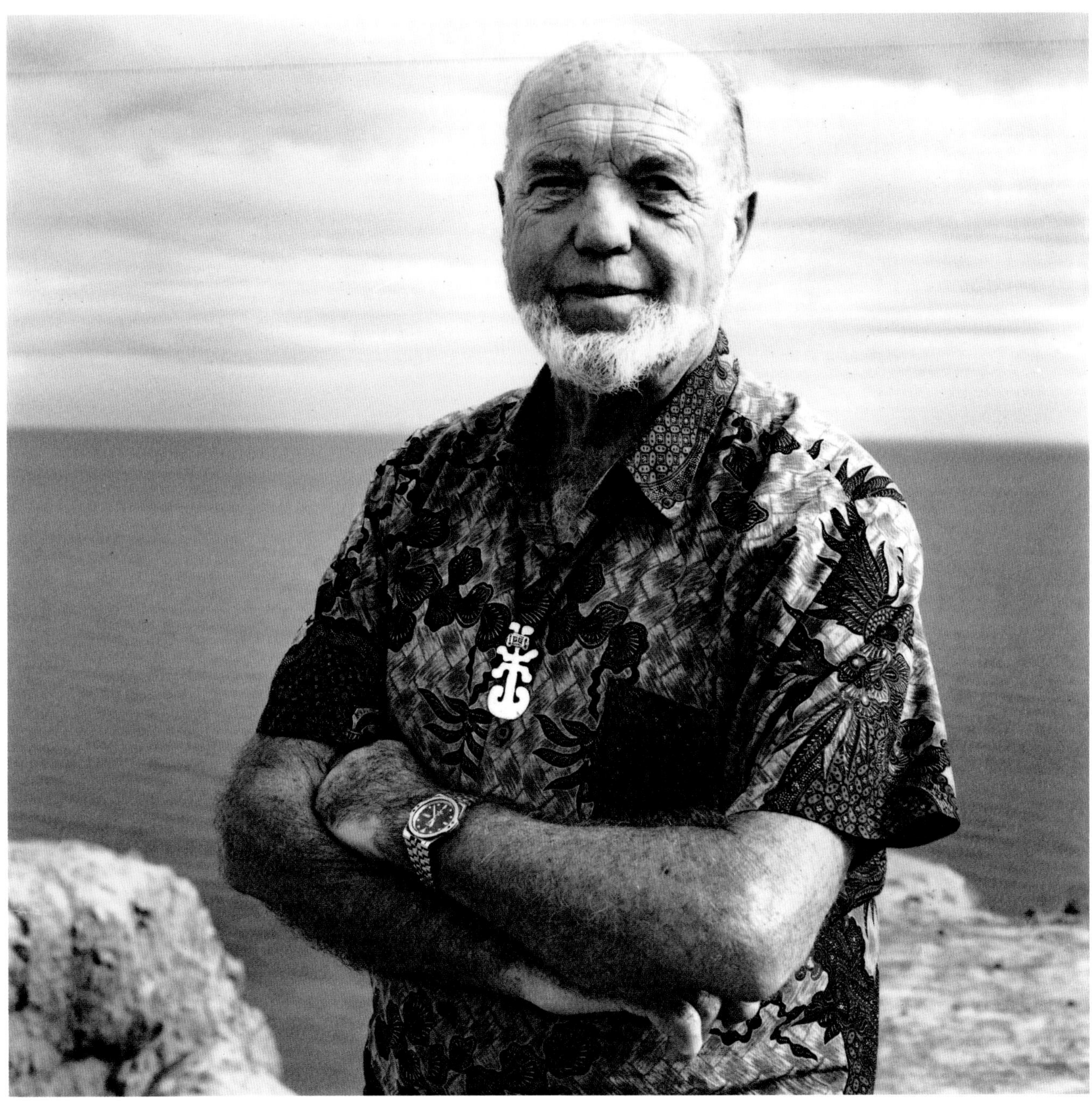

Elizabeth Gilliam (b.1942)
Photograph of Wolfgang Sievers at Half Moon Bay, Victoria 1970
gelatin silver photograph; 12.4 × 12.4cm
nla.cat-vn2121439
Courtesy Elizabeth Gilliam

Wolfgang Sievers

Helen Ennis

A Matter of Freedom: Berlin to Melbourne

When the German-born photographer Wolfgang Sievers arrived in Australia in 1938, he had already experienced several tumultuous years that affected every aspect of his life. Following Hitler's rise to power in 1933, at his father's urging, Sievers had left Berlin for Portugal. He returned to Berlin in mid-1935 to train as a photographer at the Contempora School for Applied Arts, and then fled to England in 1938 after being called up for service in the German Luftwaffe. Fortunately, however, he had already prepared to migrate to Australia (one of the sponsors for his visa was photographer Axel Poignant) and had packed up his valuable camera equipment, furniture and household items for shipment. Australia appealed to him because it was 'as far away from the Nazis as possible as well as being an English-speaking country'.[1] Within weeks of his arrival in Sydney, Sievers decided to settle in Melbourne, and in November 1938 the 35-year-old set up his business and secured his first assignments. What he offered—and what his clients appreciated from the outset—was his firsthand experience of European modernism and an international style of photography that was characterised by its objectivity, clarity and graphic impact. Through his post-war photography, especially in the architectural, industrial and mining sectors, Sievers was determined to contribute to a new vision of Australia as an industrial economy and a modern society. His aim, derived from the German Bauhaus, which was shut down by the Nazis in 1933, was to unite art and industry and pursue photography as a creative, modern enterprise.

1 All quotes from Wolfgang Sievers are derived from his commentary written to accompany his photographs in the author's National Gallery of Australia exhibition *The Life and Work of Wolfgang Sievers* (1991), a copy of which is held at the National Library of Australia, and an unpublished interview with the author (1988).

Settling into a new life in Australia was almost immediately complicated by the outbreak of the Second World War in September 1939. Sievers' initial attempts to enlist in the Australian Imperial Forces (AIF), and later in the Royal Australian Air Force (RAAF), were unsuccessful and his work as a photographer was limited to portraiture once he was classified as an enemy alien by the Australian Government (the classification applied to German immigrants living in Australia as well as immigrants from other countries that were enemies in the war). Shortly after the attack on Pearl Harbor, Sievers was finally accepted by the army and began service on 9 March 1942 as a member of the 4th Employment Company, which comprised European refugees, some of whom were Jewish. (Sievers' mother was of Jewish descent but had converted to Christianity.) Based in Albury, Sievers worked on the railways, moving stores from one train to another, due to the different rail gauges used in Victoria and New South Wales. After sustaining a spinal injury that required six months' rehabilitation, Sievers was transferred to the army headquarters' photographic section in Melbourne. There he spent nearly 18 months 'taking part in the paper war, occasionally showing an officer how to put a film into a camera and waiting for morning tea'. On 28 February 1946, Sievers was discharged from the army and resumed his photographic practice in premises at 9 Collins Street, Melbourne, where he was assisted by his Finnish wife Brita Klaerich. She had arrived in Australia in October 1939 and they had married a week later. Sievers and Klaerich had a daughter, Karin, born in 1944, and a son, Anders, born two years later.

Forgetting the Past: The Post-war Years

Sievers was naturalised as an Australian citizen in 1944, but his German background meant that he continued to attract the attention of the Australian Security Intelligence Organisation (ASIO) years afterwards. In 1954, he was investigated for possible links to the Australian Communist Party (none were found), which resulted in an illuminating report. Mr Sievers, the investigator noted,

> *is not very forthcoming in conversation & obviously is very careful to keep his real views to himself. What his views are, therefore I do not know. I did gain the impression that he could be very slightly to the left. He seems very happy in Australia and the life here appeals to him, especially the general air of 'freedom'. Altogether he is somewhat of an enigma. Undoubtedly a*

clever person, who gives the impression of having everything well assessed. Mrs S & the children most pleasant. 26/3/56.[2]

Like every other migrant, Sievers had to contend with the complex relationships between his country of origin and his new home country, and his photography represented a kind of double vision. Sievers was fiercely proud of his ancestry and his upbringing in a liberal, well-educated family; his father Johannes was a distinguished architectural and art historian, and his mother Herma oversaw a film institute.[3] However, his feelings about Germany were deeply ambivalent—he did not return for a visit until 1955—and he was endlessly grateful for the 'life, happiness and freedom' Australia had given him. Paradoxically, Sievers' German background conferred advantages; it embodied rich historical and cultural traditions, and a progressive attitude to modernity and photography that set him apart from his Australian contemporaries. Sievers' situation was not uncommon. As Margaret Garlake commented in relation to the experiences of artists exiled to Great Britain, they brought with them:

deeply held beliefs in the social role of art, the nature of artistic practice and the balance between tradition and modernity that were either ahead of thinking in this country or sufficiently distinctive to act as models for change.[4]

During his first few years in Australia, Sievers dismissed most of the photography he came across as being '50 years behind the times'. Max Dupain in Sydney and Athol Shmith in Melbourne were the only photographers whom he felt displayed some understanding of the modern era.

Although he may not have conceived them as such, Sievers developed strategies that enabled him to thrive in a new country and culture. Forging productive personal and professional relationships with other Europeans, especially Germans and Austrians, was one of them. These fellow émigrés included architect Frederick Romberg and designer Gerard Herbst, who served

2 National Archives of Australia: Australian Security Intelligence Organisation, 'Wolfgang Georg Sievers', 1939–1970, NAA: A6119, 2889.

3 Herma Sievers died in 1932; Professor Johannes Sievers remained in Berlin during the war and died in 1969. Professor Sievers was an expert on the neoclassical Prussian architect Karl Friedrich Schinkel and his books were illustrated with some of his son's earliest photographs.

4 Margaret Garlake, 'A Minor Language? Three Émigré Sculptors and Their Strategies of Assimilation', in Shulamith Behr and Marian Malet (eds), *Arts in Exile in Britain 1933–1945: Politics and Cultural Identity*, Amsterdam, New York: Rodopi, 2005, p.168.

in the same Employment Company as Sievers during the war (Herbst was one of the infamous *Dunera* internees). Four of the five most important photographers working in Melbourne in the 1950s were German-born: Helmut Newton (Neustädter), Henry Talbot (Tichauer), Mark Strizic and Sievers himself.[5] All had been profoundly affected by the spread of fascism and the outbreak of war, although the circumstances of their arrival in Australia differed greatly.

The architectural and industrial commissions Sievers received were a product of the booms in construction, heavy industry and manufacturing that occurred in the post-war period.[6] Opportunities for commercial photographers were abundant, with their work being illustrated in magazines (both in feature articles and advertisements), journals and publications such as annual reports, and being presented in trade exhibitions.

ARCHITECTURAL WORK

During the 1950s and 1960s, Sievers collaborated with leading architectural firms and architects of the day. They included Yuncken Freeman; Bates, Smart and McCutcheon; and architects Frederick Romberg, Roy Grounds, Robin Boyd, Alex Jelinek and Peter McIntyre. He considered their architecture innovative because it built on the Bauhaus ideas and modernist traditions that he admired in the work of international architects Le Corbusier, Mies van der Rohe and Alvar Aalto.

Architectural commissions were diverse, involving government, corporate and private clients. Whereas his industrial photography took him all over Australia, his architectural practice was confined mainly to Melbourne. As Australia's second largest city, Melbourne was transforming itself into a modern metropolis, a process that gained a huge impetus when it was selected to host the 1956 Olympic Games. Sievers photographed many of the city's landmark civic projects, such as the Olympic Swimming Pool, and later the Sidney Myer Music Bowl and the National Gallery of Victoria.

5 For information on Mark Strizic, see 'Mark Strizic's Melbourne: In Search of Lost Time', in Mark Strizic, *Mark Strizic: Melbourne—Marvellous to Modern*, Melbourne: Thames and Hudson, in association with the State Library of Victoria, 2009, p.7. For information on Helmut Newton, see Guy Featherstone, 'Helmut Newton's Australian Years', *The La Trobe Journal*, no.76, Spring 2005, pp.105–123; and Helen Ennis, 'Don't Look Back: Helmut Newton's Australian Years', *Photofile*, no.52, December 1997, pp.10–15. Austrian-born photographer Margaret Michaelis established a studio in Sydney after arriving in Australia in 1939 and later moved to Melbourne; see Helen Ennis, *Margaret Michaelis: Love, Loss and Photography*, Canberra: National Gallery of Australia, 2005.

6 See Roger Benjamin, *Growing Up Modern: Canberra's Round House and Alex Jelinek*, Braddon, ACT and Ultimo, Sydney: Halstead Press, 2022.

In the residential field, Sievers worked at the high end of the market, photographing unique, architect-designed flats and houses. An early architectural assignment was for a Swiss-trained architect, Frederik Romberg, who had arrived in Melbourne in 1939. Sievers' dynamic, stylish photographs of Romberg's block of flats, 'Stanhill', in Melbourne, were published in *Art in Australia*, which championed modern architecture and modern living. Another outstanding example of domestic architecture was the Round House designed by Czechoslovakian immigrant Alex Jelinek and located in the Canberra suburb of Deakin.[7] Commissioned by Professor Bruce Benjamin and his wife Audrey, the house set a benchmark in the application of a geometrically oriented international style in an Australian setting and won the *Architecture and Arts* award, House of the Year, in 1958. Sievers' photographs of the house were featured in a prestigious international magazine, *Aujourd'hui: art et architecture* (September 1959).

Generally, Sievers' exterior views of residential buildings are more memorable than his interior shots, in part because he was so attuned to large-scale structures and expansive spaces. Most domestic interior spaces appear to have constrained him; not only were they too small, they were also too intimate. However, noteworthy shots include studies of Heide, the home at Heidelberg in Melbourne designed by David McGlashan for prominent art patrons John and Sunday Reed (now the Heide Museum of Modern Art).

From the 1960s onwards, Sievers' architectural work was dominated by commissions from the high end of town. The newly completed high-rise buildings—which epitomised Melbourne's modernisation and occurred with little resistance or criticism at the time—were the headquarters for insurance companies, banks, corporations and mining companies. Most of these buildings were in the international style of architecture that Sievers mirrored in his own functionalist, objective photography emphasising rationality and efficiency. His images spoke not only the language of architecture, but also the language of modern capitalism. Their tone was assured and authoritative.

In contrast to domestic architecture, high-rise buildings gave Sievers large interior spaces—entrances, foyers, open-plan offices—to work with. The images convey a good deal of information about conditions for the rapidly growing numbers of clerical staff in the 1960s

7 See Isobel Crombie, '"Industralia": Wolfgang Sievers', in Ann Stephens, Philip Goad and Andrew McNamara (eds), *Modern Times: The Untold Story of Modernism in Australia*, Melbourne: Miegunyah Press, 2008.

and the hierarchical structure within which they worked. On many occasions, Sievers set up the camera as far back as possible, to provide an expansive view that emphasises the repeated patterns of modular workspaces, which are separated from managers' offices and boardrooms. Such images give an overwhelming impression of uniformity and, by implication, of conformity. People are mostly absent, the brand-new workplaces not yet displaying any signs of human occupation or personalisation.

By the early 1970s, Sievers declared himself very dissatisfied with the quality of contemporary architecture—he rejected a request to photograph the new Parliament House in Canberra because he considered the architecture to be 'appallingly bad'—and began to focus on industrial and mining photography instead.

AN INDUSTRIAL LENS

Sievers' early training in Germany, where he developed his grasp of structure and form, and his reverence for the machine age bore outstanding dividends in his industrial photography. His output was diverse and included photographs of buildings and plants associated with industry, manufacturing processes, products and the inter-related area of work, undertaken for clients based in the timber, paper, chemical, glass and textile industries.

Industrial photography was the area in which Sievers made a particularly original and long-lasting contribution—in part because of the clarity of his vision of Australia as a modern, industrial economy no longer solely dependent on its earlier agricultural base. His photographs were used in Australia in annual reports and promotional material, but their international reach was also crucial; through their presentation in trade exhibitions and publications that promoted exports, the photographs had a larger role in changing people's perceptions of Australia. As Sievers explained, his primary concern was:

> *to promote and enhance Australia's standing in the world as an industrial nation capable of turning out precision work of the highest quality and to overcome ideas still widely held overseas that Australia was a strange place only fit for sheep, wheat, minerals, kangaroos* (1988)

The photographs' clarity and graphic power demand attention.

The ambitiousness of the post-war role for Australian industry was matched by the boldness of Sievers' approach to industrial photography. It was here that he could be simultaneously at his most imaginative and masterful. In his hands, industrial photography became a thoroughly creative enterprise, displaying his distinctive vision that was at once theatrical, futuristic and impersonal. Over time, it also became increasingly grand. Sievers' achievements did not relate simply to his love of industry, but to his appreciation of good design that triumphed in the industrial sphere. Everything he depicted—whether buildings, machinery or products—related to function, with nothing extraneous or excessive included.

As early as the 1950s, Sievers was revelling in the creative possibilities provided by large industrial complexes, in images that conveyed a sense of almost limitless scale, far beyond the human. On the rare occasion workers were included in outdoor shots, they were dwarfed by their surroundings. Sievers was also captivated by the modern materials used in construction and wrote in 1988 that:

Photographing an oil refinery is sheer delight: the concentration of pure forms in shining aluminium present a wonderful challenge to the eye and the mind of a photographer.

His images of factory interiors were equally spectacular, often rendered with an extraordinary depth of field, which ensures that objects in the immediate foreground and far distance have the same exactitude, giving the viewer a full view of the immensity and complexity of the operations being pictured.

When photographing factory interiors and manufacturing processes, Sievers' intellectual approach came to the fore. There was nothing intuitive or spontaneous about the images he made; they were imagined beforehand and carefully constructed. Elaborate and time-consuming measures were frequently involved: cleaning up the factory, moving equipment around, erecting scaffolding to secure the best vantage point and so on. Sievers preferred working at night when the factory floor could be transformed into something akin to a film set and animated through the creative use of lighting. He stated that:

The majority of my work in factories was carried out at nighttime in order to eliminate unsightly background or the dreadful sawtooth corrugated iron roof structures. Working out of darkness and illuminating the scene with my own few light sources gave me the dramatic effects I wanted (1988)

This ideas-based approach was behind the making of his most famous work, *Gears for the Mining Industry, Vickers Ruwolt, Burnley, Victoria* (1967), which he has described in detail as an exemplar:

of what can happen when one's imagination is set to work. I thought I might be able to create a symbolic photograph of Australia's engineering skills to show the world outside that Australia was not merely a continent of raw materials.

So I moved into the factory around seven in the evening and started the long process of tidying up, moving, arranging and setting up meticulous lighting without interfering with the factory's normal production. There was a foreman and an engineer with me and a crane to stand one half upright then suspend the other above it in an inverted position. Finally the engineer was asked to measure the teeth of the gears—technically quite a dubious performance, but added to give an idea of scale. (1988)

While *Gears for the Mining Industry* might symbolise Australia's engineering and manufacturing skills, the scene Sievers created is fantastical—or, in his own words, 'a fake'. The gears do not, and cannot, work in the configuration realised for the photograph. Although Sievers' working processes were time-consuming and exacting, he stressed that his photographic technique was straightforward and that he did not utilise any special techniques in the darkroom, 'everything is stock standard if only meticulous in execution'.

Another highly successful strand of Sievers' industrial work built on his love for 'the thing itself'. This can be seen in images both of machines and their mass-produced products that exclude any reference to either a human presence or a human dimension. The beauty and functionality of objects in all their diversity are stressed; whether a stone crusher, storage tanks, a stack of paper, wool bobbins, or groups of bronze pipes and castings, all are given a rapt kind of attention and rendered with precision.

In Sievers' own assessment, the relationship between 'man and machine' was at the crux of his contribution to industrial photography. He admired fine craftsmanship and through his images of workers argued for the dignity of labour, which was often expressed in terms of the contact between the workman and his tools or the products with whose manufacture he was involved. These anonymous skilled workers—their face and hands sometimes touched with light—are represented as heroes of the modern age.

By the mid-1960s, however, Sievers was faced with the loss of his favoured subject because of the advent of an increasingly mechanised and automated work environment. The centrepiece of modern manufacturing was the assembly line and the reality for workers involved in mass production was highly repetitive operations. There is nothing inspiring about Sievers' images of workers on the production line, whether it is women checking for imperfections in runs of fabric or packing tins of shoe polish. Indeed, it can be argued that Sievers photographed manufacturing at a key moment of transition as skilled workers became increasingly irrelevant and then were displaced altogether. He recalled that, by the 1960s, factories, which were once filled with people, had become almost empty, commonly run by a computer system and only a few operators.

MINING AND MORALITY

The halcyon days of Sievers' architectural and industrial photography were the 1950s and 1960s. From the 1970s onwards, he focussed on the mining industries (bauxite, coal, minerals, oil) that had earlier been only one aspect of his practice. As he explained it, he 'did not relinquish industrial photography'; he 'merely transferred it from the factory halls into the open air'. His approach to mining revelled in scenes that went beyond human scale and inspired awe.[8] *'Curtains of Fire', Shell's Drilling Rig, the 'Nymphea' in Bass Strait, Victoria* (1983) was one of the most stunning photographs of his career—deep red, full of theatre and conveying an extraordinary sense of scale. Here, the human dimension is all but subsumed into an operatic display of the power and might of industrial forces.

Sievers was far more than an impartial recorder of the achievements of industry and mining. He was responsive to his clients' interests and was a forceful advocate for their respective sectors.

8 For a corollary, see Edward Burtynsky's Western Australian work in Helen Ennis, 'Edward Burtynsky's Minescapes: An Australian Perspective', in Ray Coffey (ed.), *Edward Burtynsky: Australian Minescapes*, Perth: Western Australian Museum, 2009.

This interdependence raises important ethical and moral issues, some of which Sievers himself began to publicly acknowledge late in his career:

> *I am quite aware of the moral problems confronting a responsible photographer in industry. Should he be working for multinational companies at all if he believes—as I do—that Australia should have retained 51% ownership of its resources? Should he use his skills to hide the terrible pollution and despoliation of our country—as I have? In creating beautiful images I have glamorized industries which have often been heedless of their sacred trust to use resources wisely and take care in the interest of future generations. In my defence, so far, I have found no valid answer to these problems.*

It was not only pollution and despoliation of the natural environment, which he referred to, that resulted from mining activities in Australia. They also impacted on Aboriginal people living in areas rich with mineral resources. In 1957, while on assignment for Comalco at Weipa on Cape York in northern Queensland, Sievers took several photographs of Aboriginal people at the Methodist Mission. Using a documentary style, they depict everyday activities—going to the shop or to church, receiving health care and so on. The photograph he titled *Aboriginal 'Black Madonna', Weipa, Cape York, North Queensland*, which represents a young Aboriginal woman holding a baby, is an overwhelmingly positive image of maternal care.

The photography Sievers undertook for the giant mining and oil companies—Australian and multinational—upheld their activities and values, but he expressed some radical beliefs in other areas of his life. In 1970, his actions brought him to the attention of ASIO once more when, according to an Intercept Report on his file, he sought material on the Vietnam Moratorium campaign to display in the showcase window of his business. A gruesome *Life* magazine photograph of a soldier holding part of a dead body was accompanied by the following statement:

> *I Wolfgang Sievers, victim of Nazi persecution, prisoner of the Gestapo, volunteer AIF and RAAF 1939, volunteer Australian Army 1941–45, PROTEST against this undeclared war, against conscription by lottery, against imprisonment of conscientious objectors whose just stand has been laid down at the Nuremberg Trials to be the duty of all men.*

The declaration of his anti-war beliefs apparently cost him several major clients.

In the last years of his life, Sievers devoted himself to researching the lives of Nazi war criminals who had found refuge in Australia, gathering evidence for the Australian Government's investigation into war crimes and for the Simon Wiesenthal Jewish Documentation Center in Vienna. In *The Australian Jewish News* on 20 September 1991, he explained his motivations as follows:

> *To me, freedom and tolerance and understanding of racism ... [are] the most basic thing[s] in life. My great task is to educate the younger generation that the wartime criminals can't get away with it and will eventually be brought to justice.*

Legacy

To understand both the distinctive nature and significance of Sievers' contribution, the context of modernism is also important—especially as it relates to Australian photographic history and practice. While crossovers exist between Sievers' work and that of his modernist peers, his approach differed in crucial ways. He never made a distinction between professional and exhibition photography (what we would now call art photography) and was unconcerned with developing an Australian aesthetic that prioritised distinctively Australian subject matter and features, including the quality of light. Nor was self-expression a motive: his photographs were produced on commission and were not invested with the same kind of subjectivity as the art photography of his Australian-born peers.

Like other European émigrés working in Australia, Sievers' internationalist vision found expression in an international style. His architectural and industrial photographs look like they could have been taken anywhere in the industrial world, and yet, their reality is more nuanced than that. Sievers passionately identified with Australia and celebrated the different kinds of freedom it offered; for example, he felt able to work more creatively in Australian workplaces because he found them more egalitarian than in class-conscious Germany. Further, his photography conveyed a well-articulated nationalistic agenda—helping position Australia as a modern, industrial economy.

A consequence of Sievers' European-based approach, which put art in the service of industry, was that his work did not appear on the art exhibition circuit but rather in trade exhibitions.

He mounted only one independent exhibition while working as a professional photographer—*New Visions in Photography*, which he held jointly with Helmut Newton at the Federal Hotel in Melbourne in 1953. The photographers' aim was 'to demonstrate ... the potential of industrial and fashion photography as a means of better promotion and bigger sales in business today'. In the 1970s, Sievers' photography began to be collected by art museums and, by the 1980s, it had finally begun to attract considerable scholarly and popular attention. In 1991, it was featured in the National Gallery of Australia's touring exhibition *The Life and Work of Wolfgang Sievers* (which I curated),[9] and is now routinely included in major group exhibitions of Australian photography. In recognition of his achievements in the fields of industrial and architectural photography, Sievers was appointed an Officer of the Order of Australia in 2002.

While Sievers' output did not fit readily into conventional narratives of Australian art photography, its 'difference' has been greatly beneficial, helping expand ideas about creative photographic practice and modernism, and the appreciation of modernism as encompassing a myriad of responses to the conditions of modernity.

The Modern Age

Only a tiny fraction of Wolfgang Sievers' vast output appears in this book but his great command of his medium and its language is clear throughout. Much of what Sievers photographed no longer exists materially; the high-rise buildings, factories, plant and machinery have disappeared or become superseded. But even more profound is the loss of something far less tangible, the faith in the modern age and its spirit that underpins Sievers' work. This has been vanquished through the rise of more complex and contradictory attitudes to technology, the occurrence of countless environmental catastrophes and the rapid pace of climate change. Sievers' photography declares its faith in technology as a beneficent force. This, more than anything, relates the images to their own times, not our own.

---

9 Jorge Calado curated a major one-person exhibition of Sievers' work in 2000. *Linha de Vida: A Fotografia de Wolfgang Sievers 1933–1993*, which included a strong component of his Portuguese photography, was held at the Arquivo Fotografico Municipal de Lisboa. See also, Naomi Cass and Kyla McFarlane, *The Sievers Project*, Melbourne: Centre for Contemporary Photography, 2014.

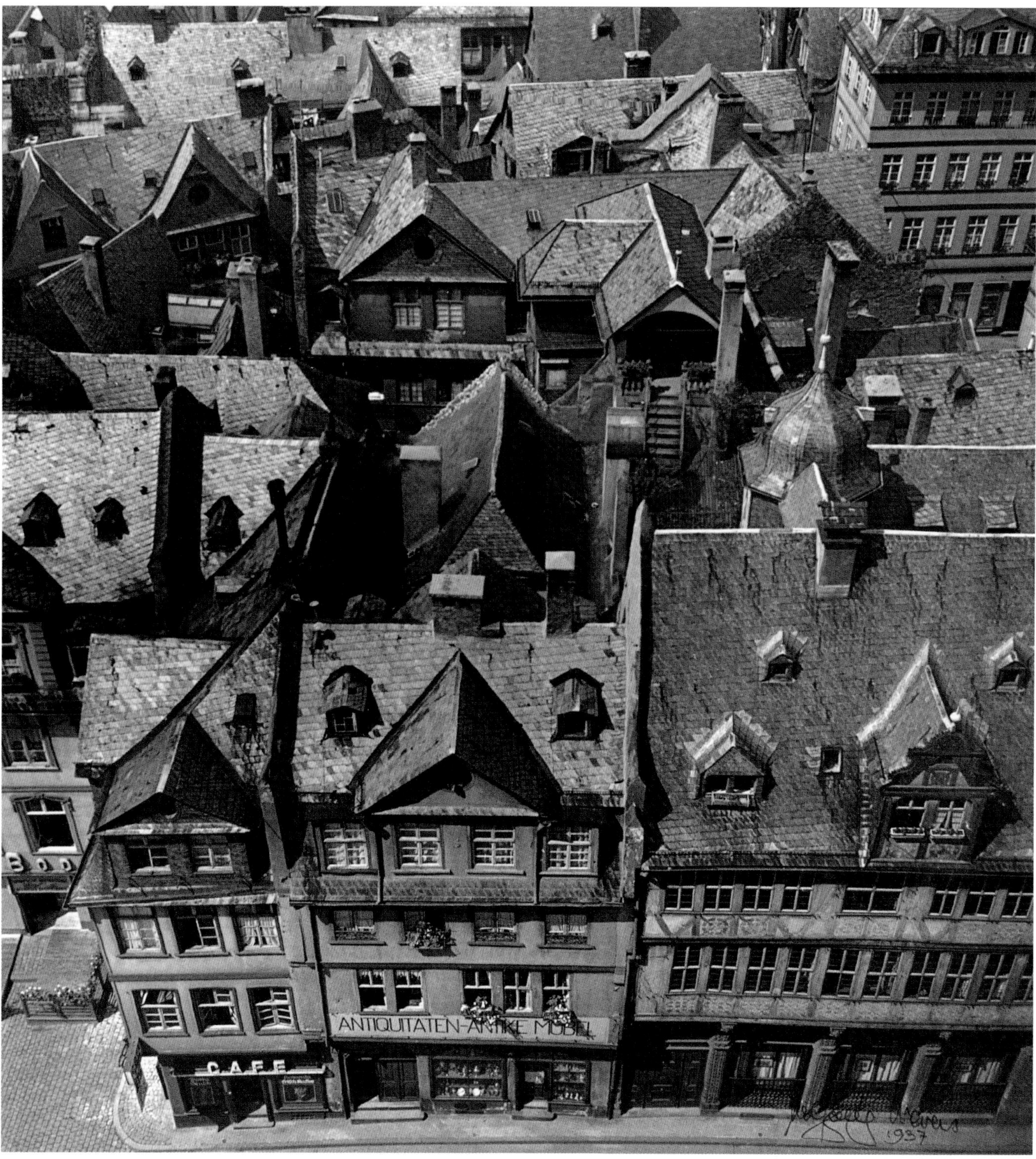

Old Frankfurt, Germany 1937
gelatin silver photograph; 39.4 × 44cm
nla.cat-vn2543401

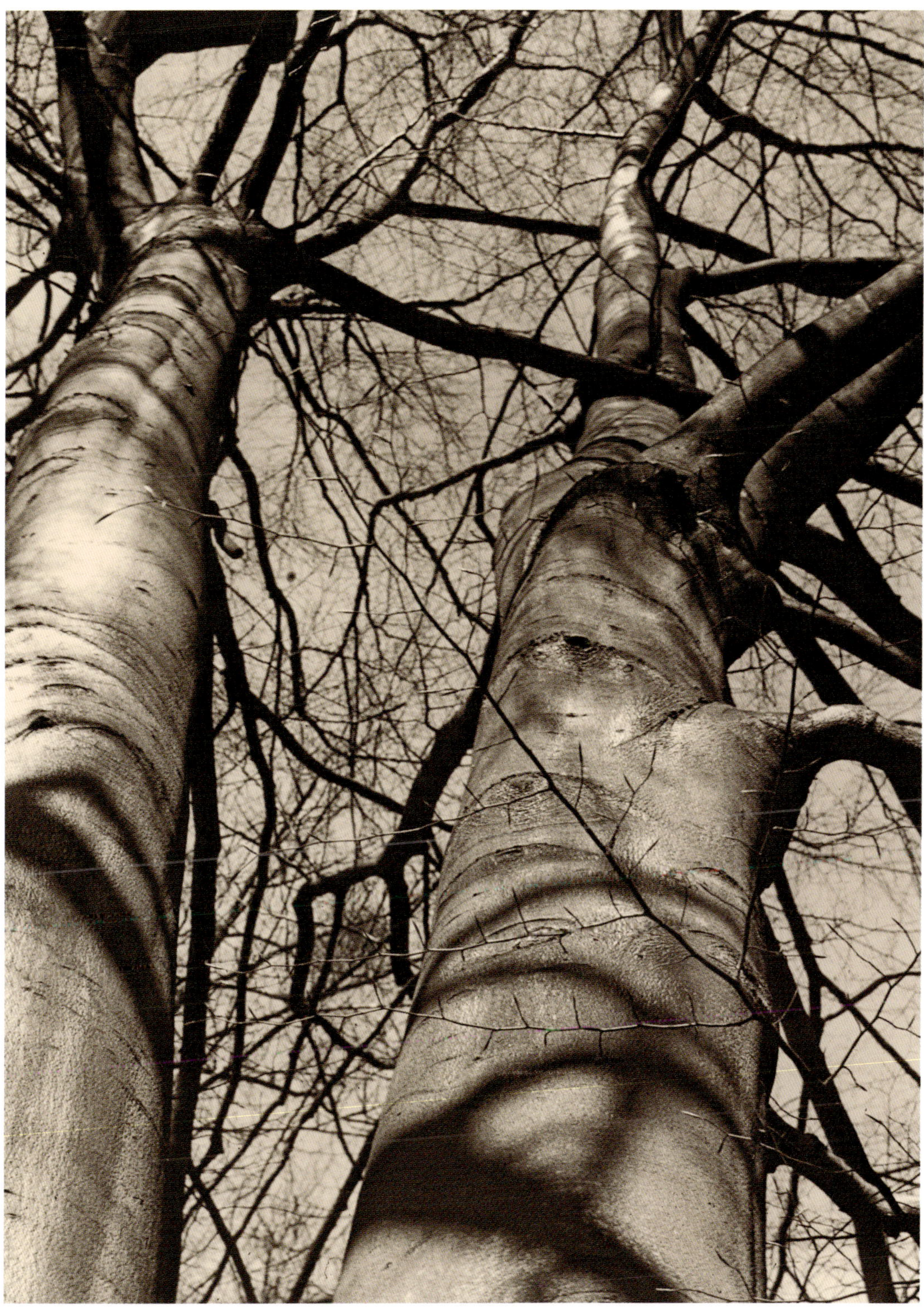

Birch Trees in the Park of Schloss Glienicke Near Berlin, Germany 1937
gelatin silver photograph; 22.3 × 28.9cm
nla.cat-vn2539906

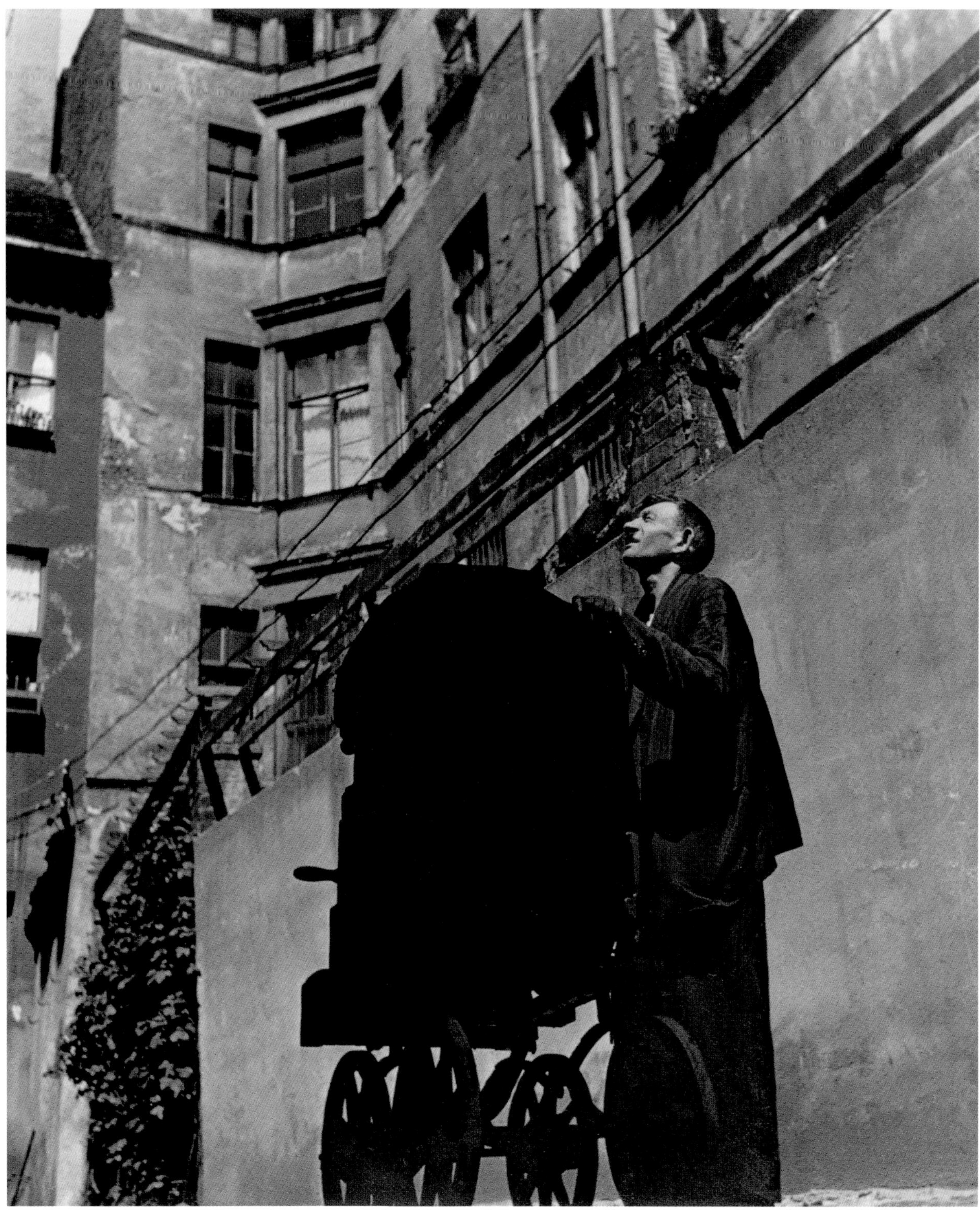

Poverty in Berlin, Germany 1933
gelatin silver photograph; 29.2 × 36cm
nla.cat-vn2536969

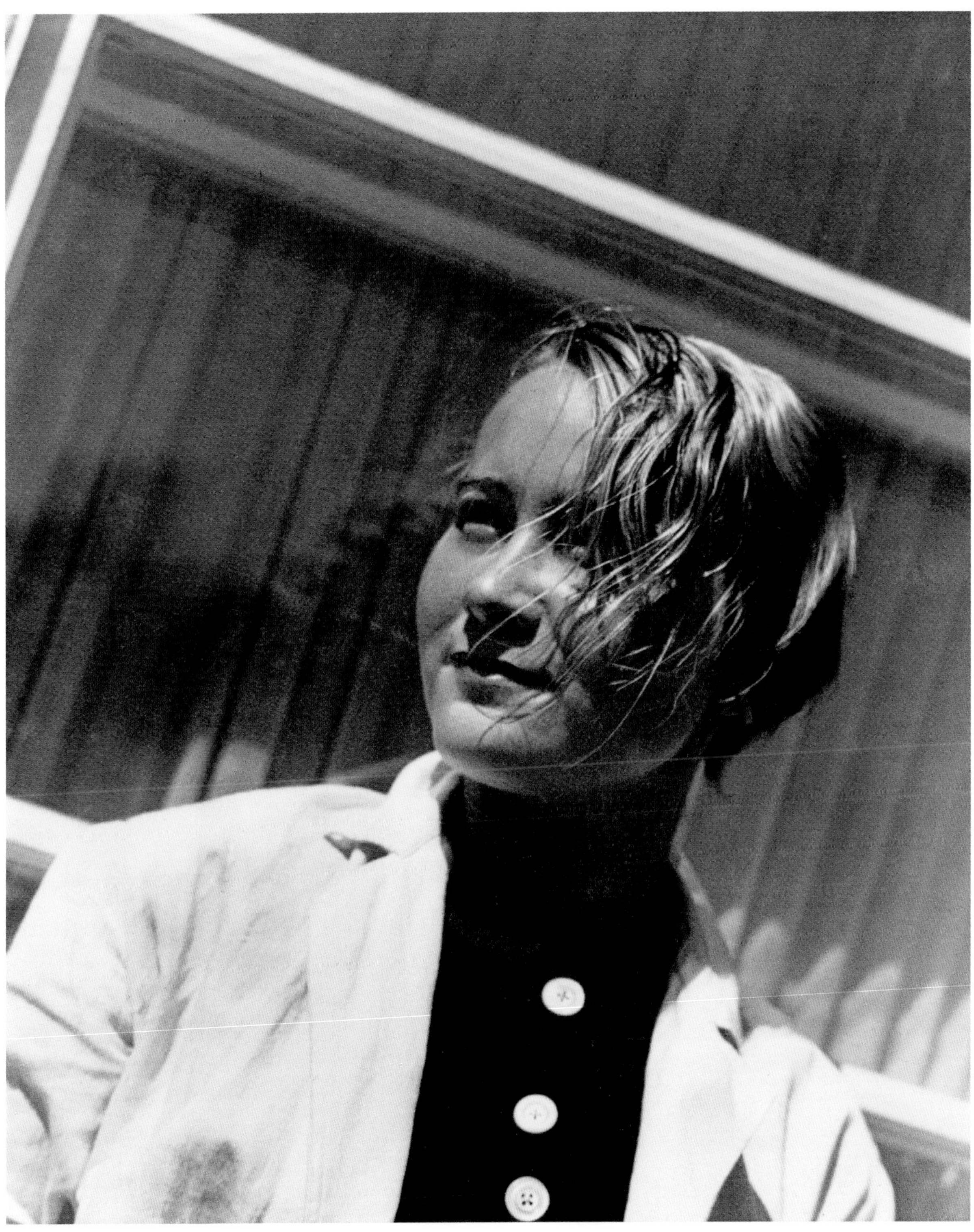

Asta von Borch, Student at the Contempora School for Applied Arts, Berlin, Germany 1937
gelatin silver photograph; 29.2 × 36.7cm
nla.cat-vn1014010

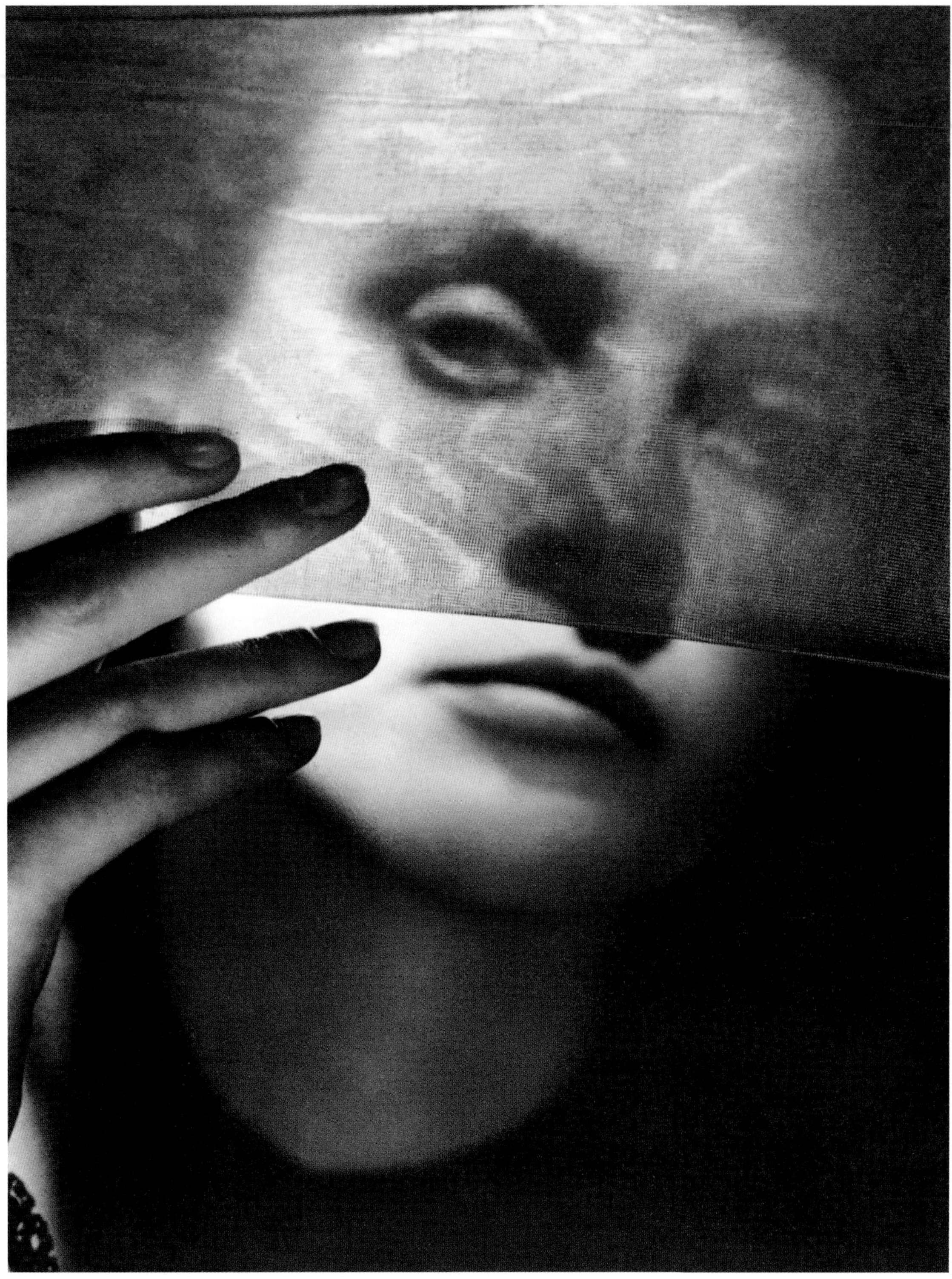

'Elbeo' Stockings Advertisement, Contempora School for Applied Arts, Berlin, Germany 1938
gelatin silver photograph; 28.9 × 38.9cm
nla.cat-vn1014330

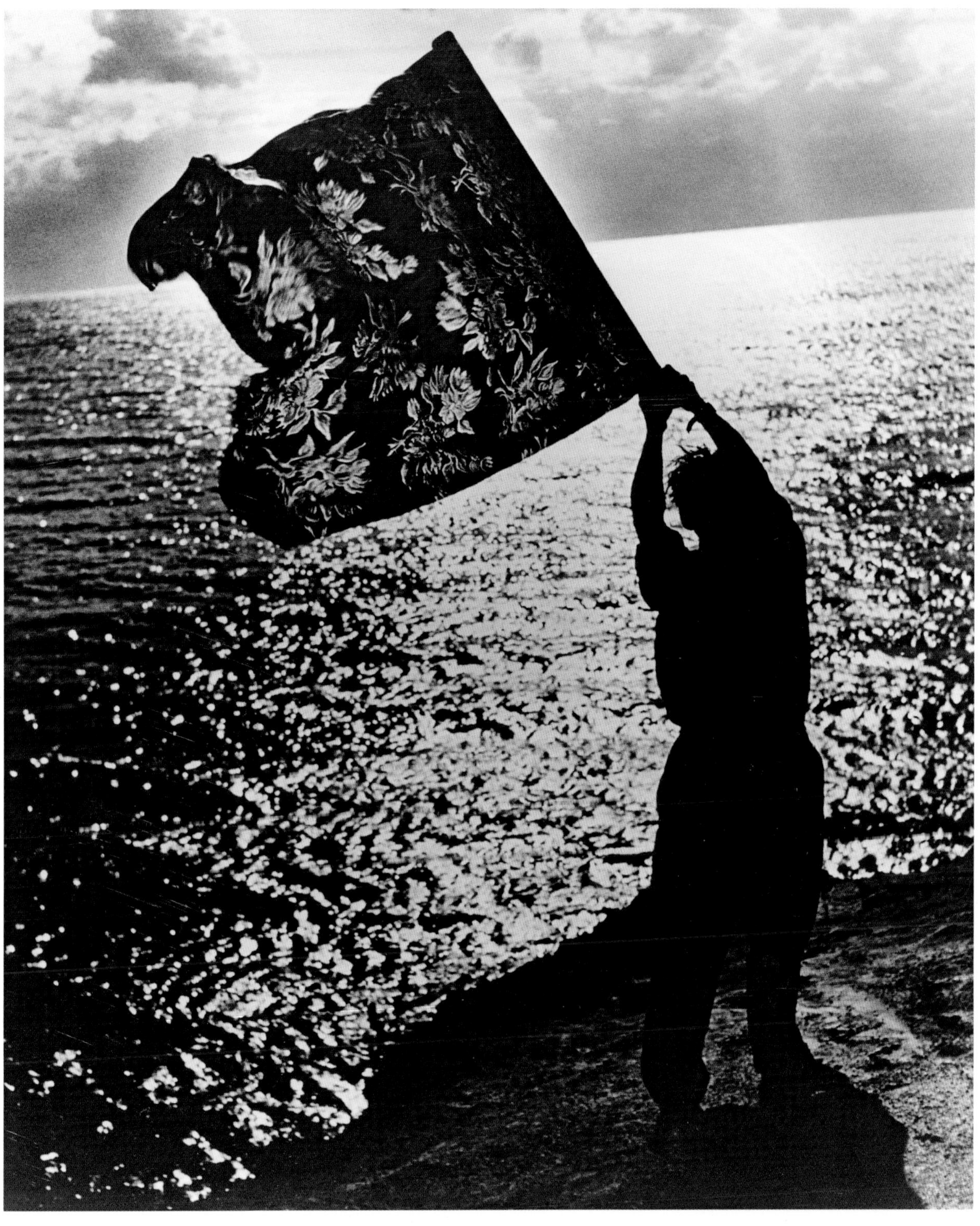

The Designer Gerard Herbst with His Design of Prestige Material at Red Bluff, Victoria 1950
gelatin silver photograph; 50.1 × 40.3cm
nla.cat-vn707664

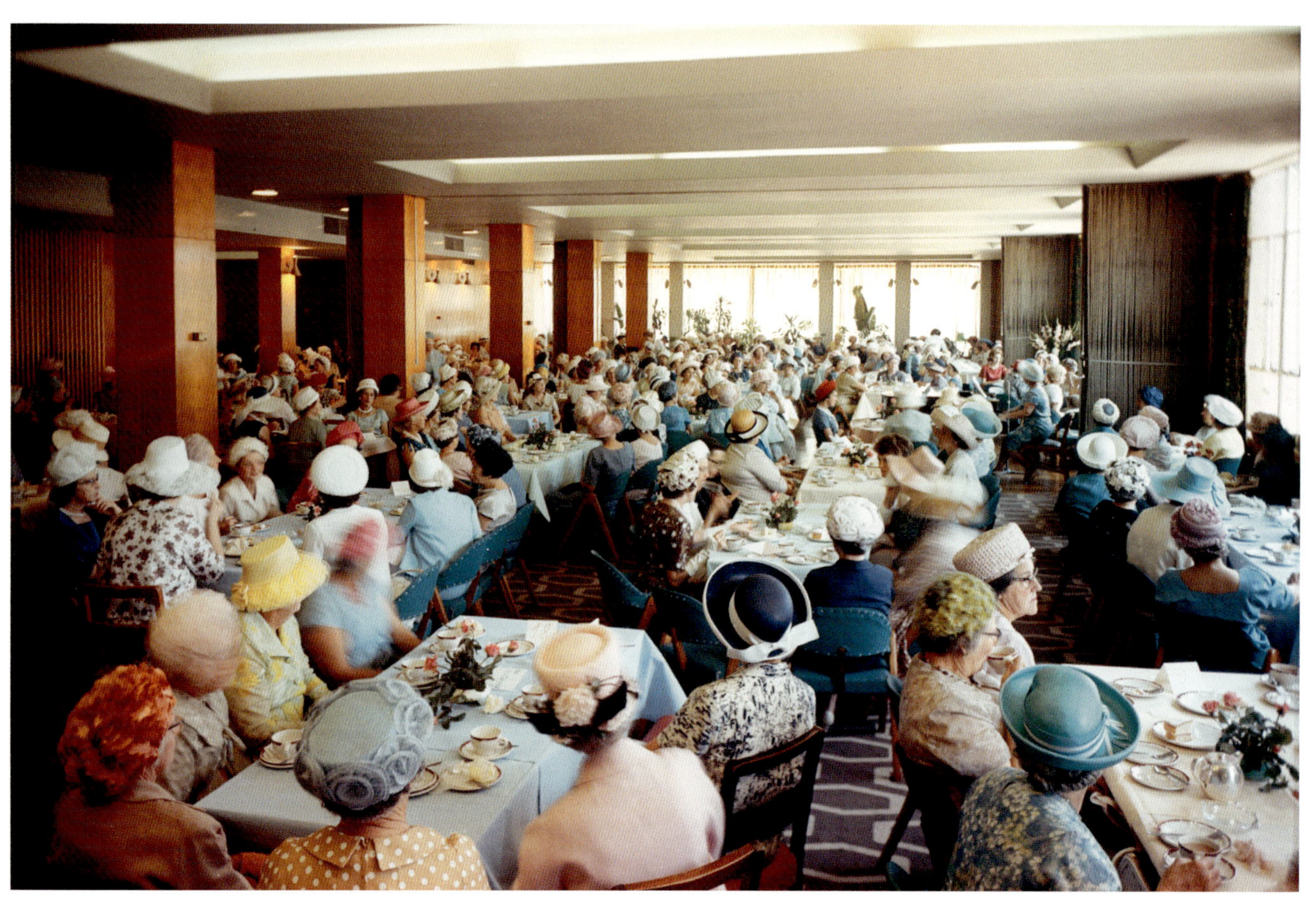

Country Women's Association Meeting at Lennons Hotel, Brisbane, Queensland 1965
type C photograph; 50.3 × 34.1cm
nla.cat-vn2513616

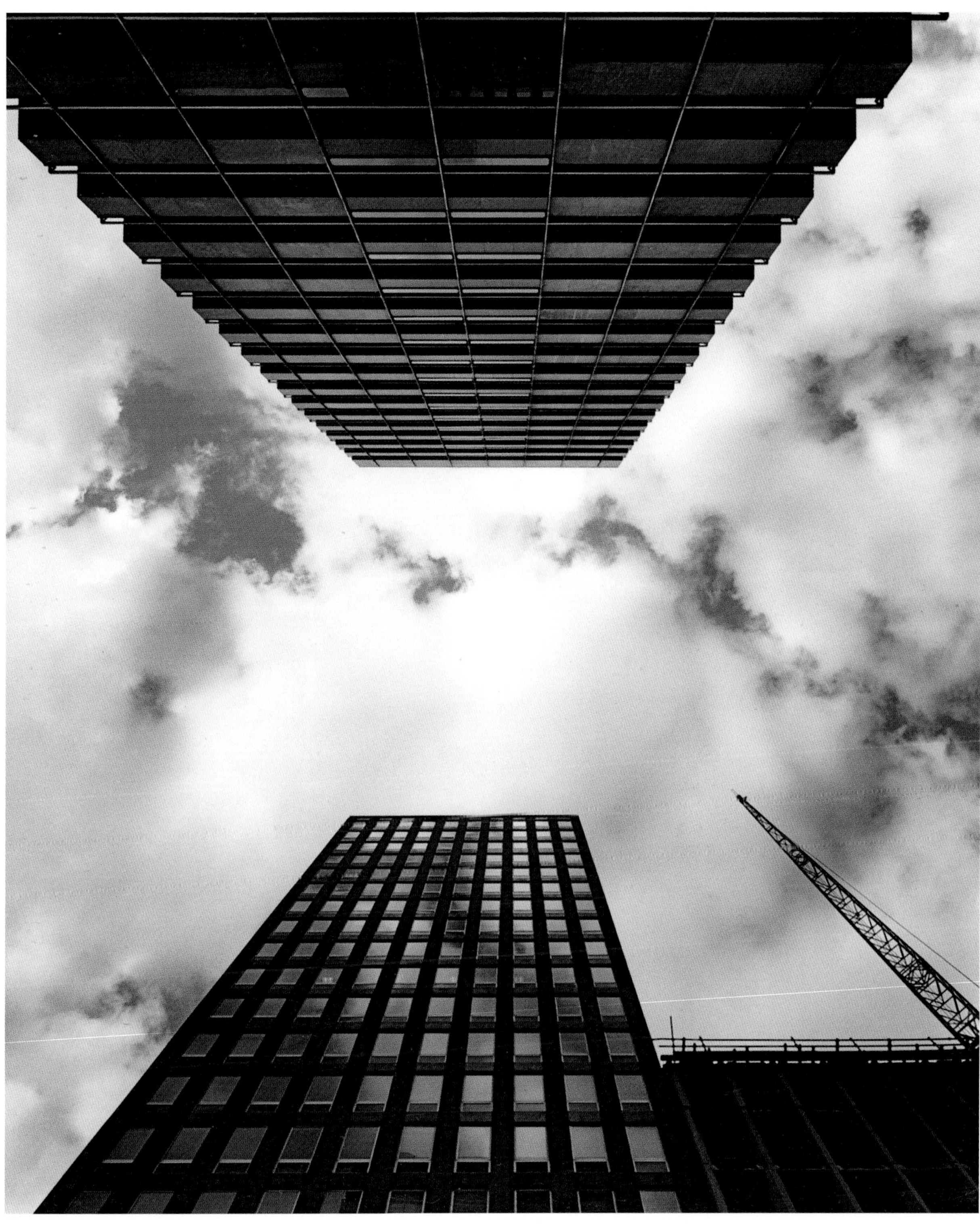

[Looking Toward the Sky] between Two Buildings in William Street, Melbourne, Victoria 1968
gelatin silver photograph; 24.5 × 19.8cm
nla.cat-vn3359899

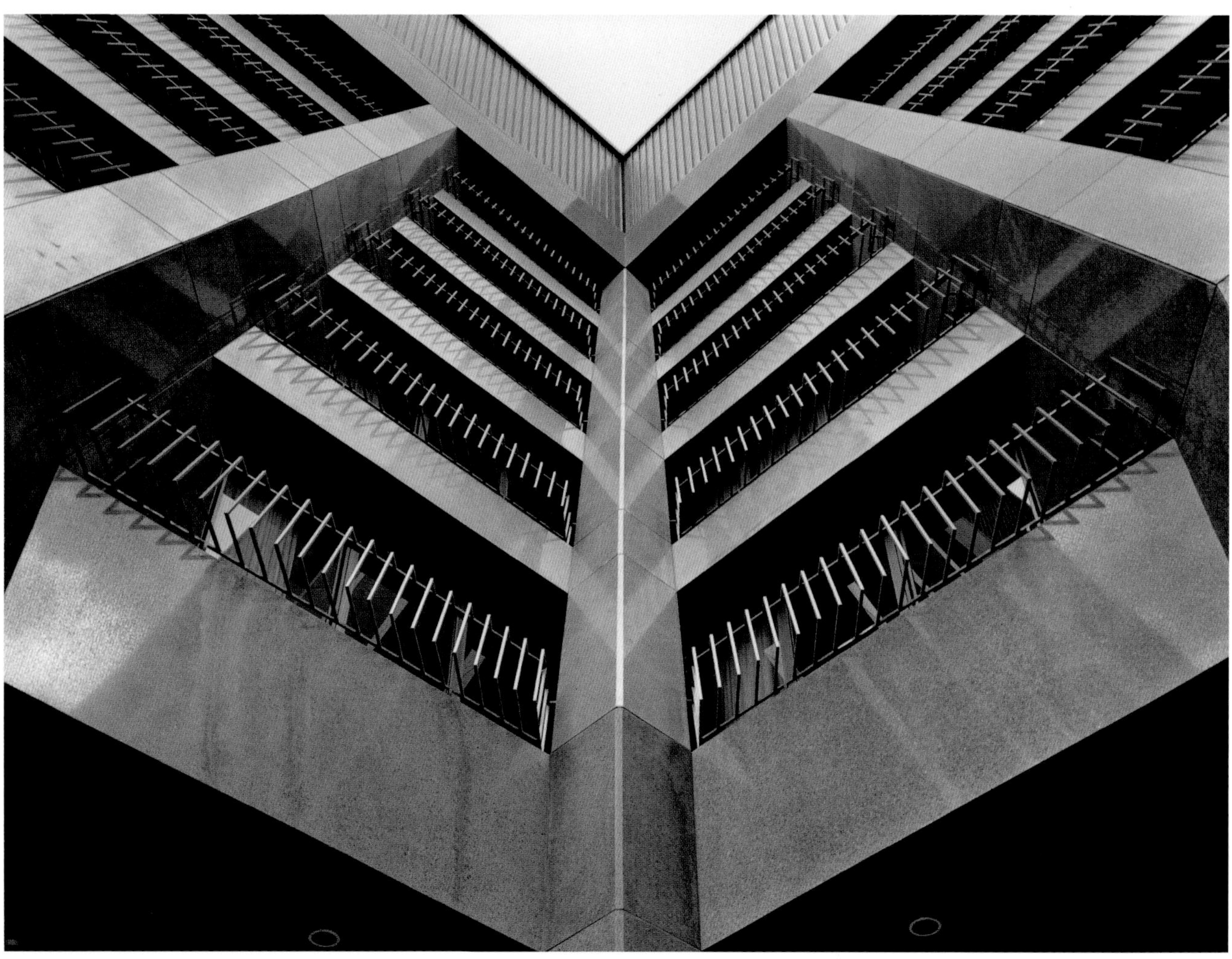

Exterior of AMP Offices, Melbourne, Victoria 1970
gelatin silver photograph; 19.5 × 25.3cm
nla.cat-vn3967962

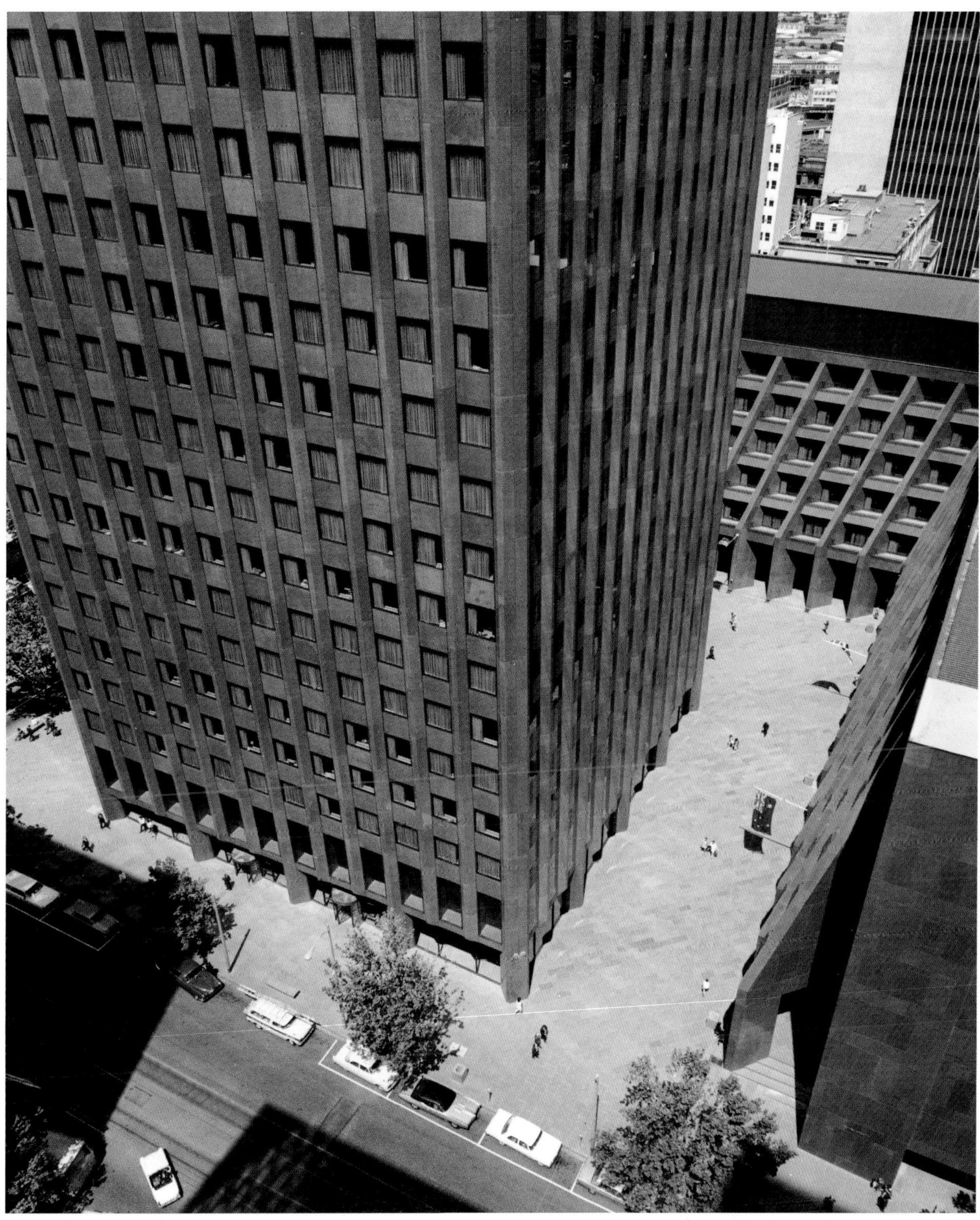

Exterior of AMP Offices, Melbourne, Victoria 1970
gelatin silver photograph; 21 × 25cm
nla.cat-vn2266851

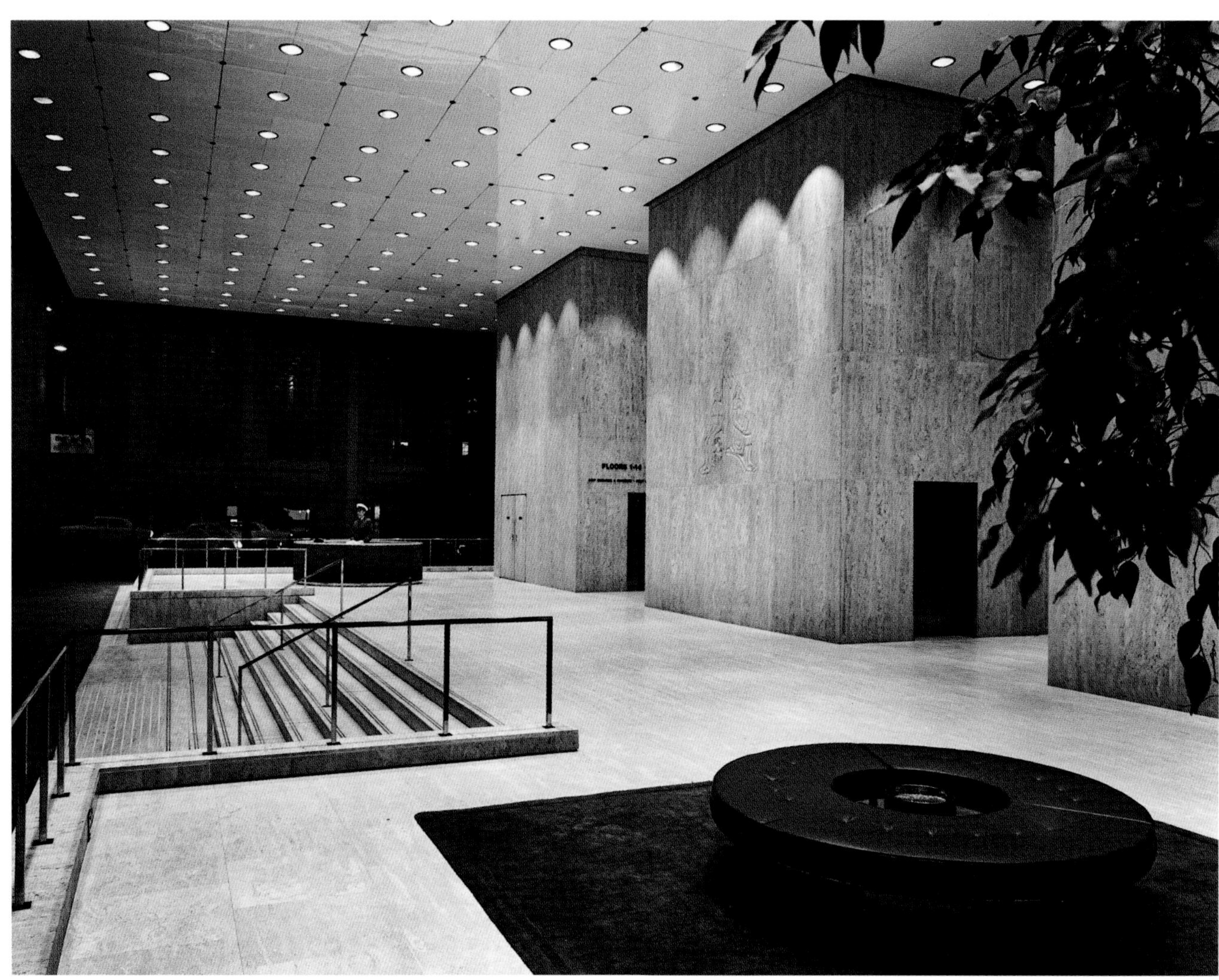

Foyer of AMP Offices, Melbourne, Victoria 1970
gelatin silver photograph; 21 × 25cm
nla.cat-vn2266323

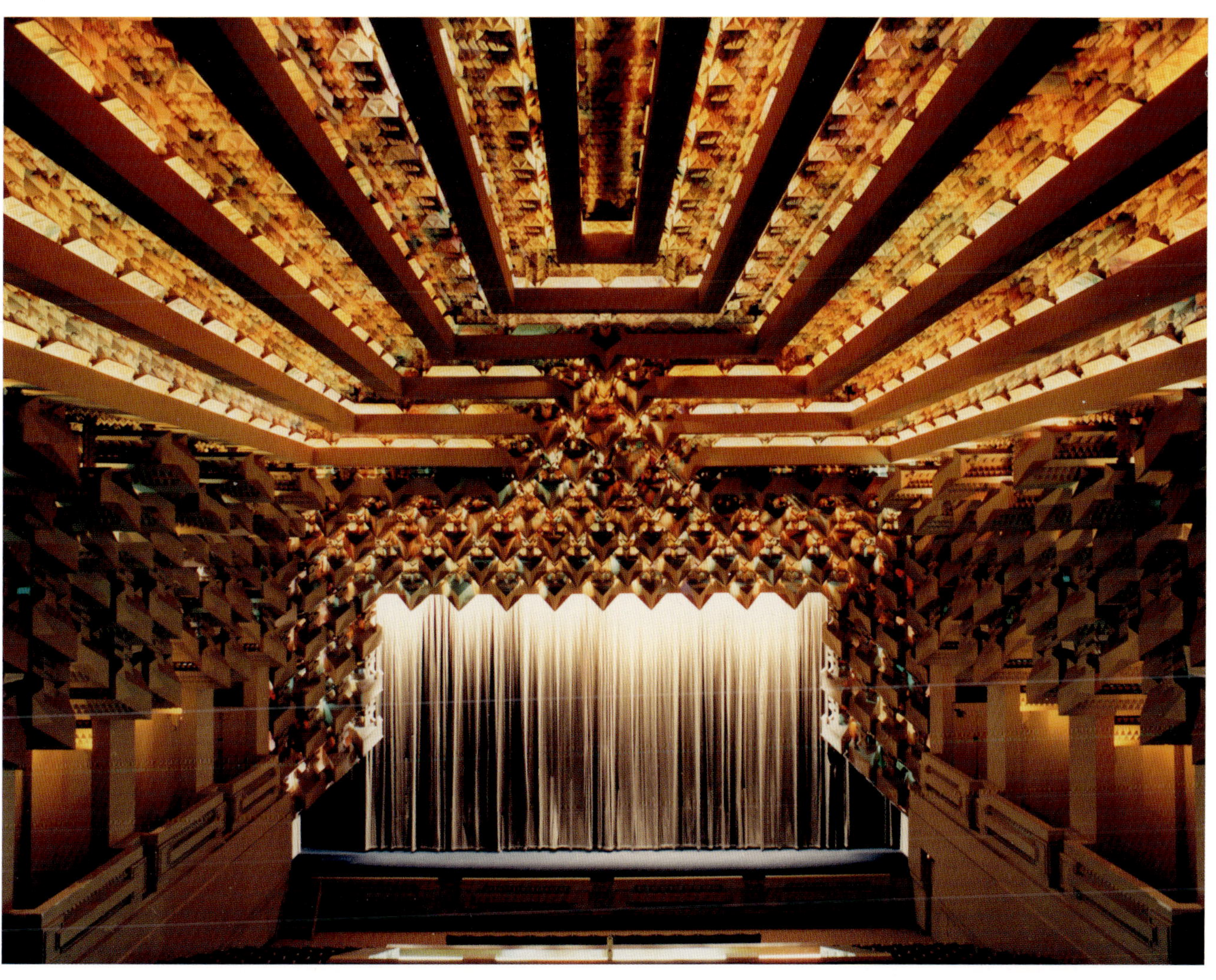

Interior of Capitol Theatre, Capitol House, Melbourne, Victoria, Ceiling Designed by Marion Mahony Griffin 1975
type C photograph; 21 × 25cm
nla.cat-vn2289291

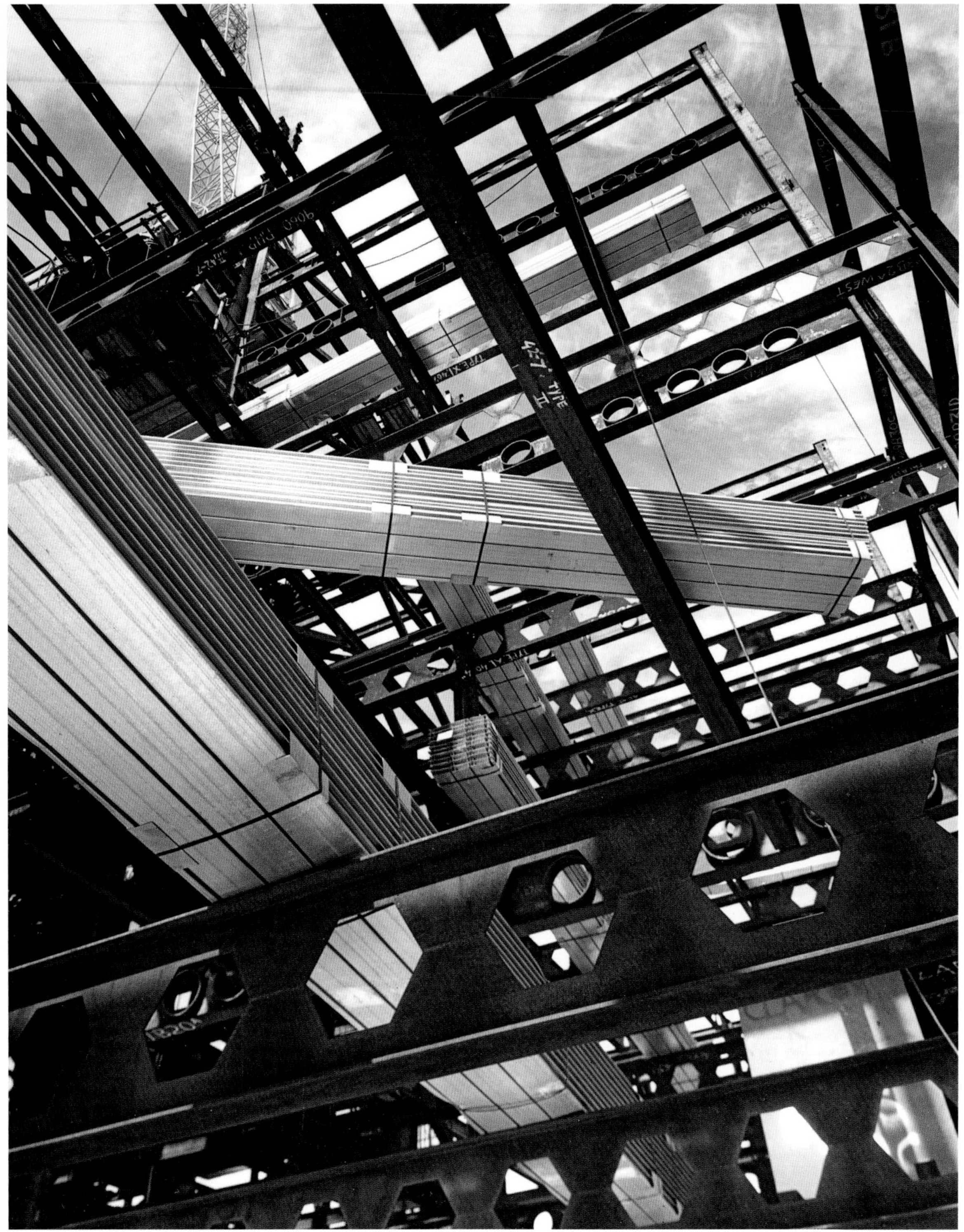

Construction of the Former BHP House, 140 William Street, Melbourne, Victoria, Architects Yuncken Freeman 1971
gelatin silver photograph; 25.2 × 19.5cm
nla.cat-vn3008225

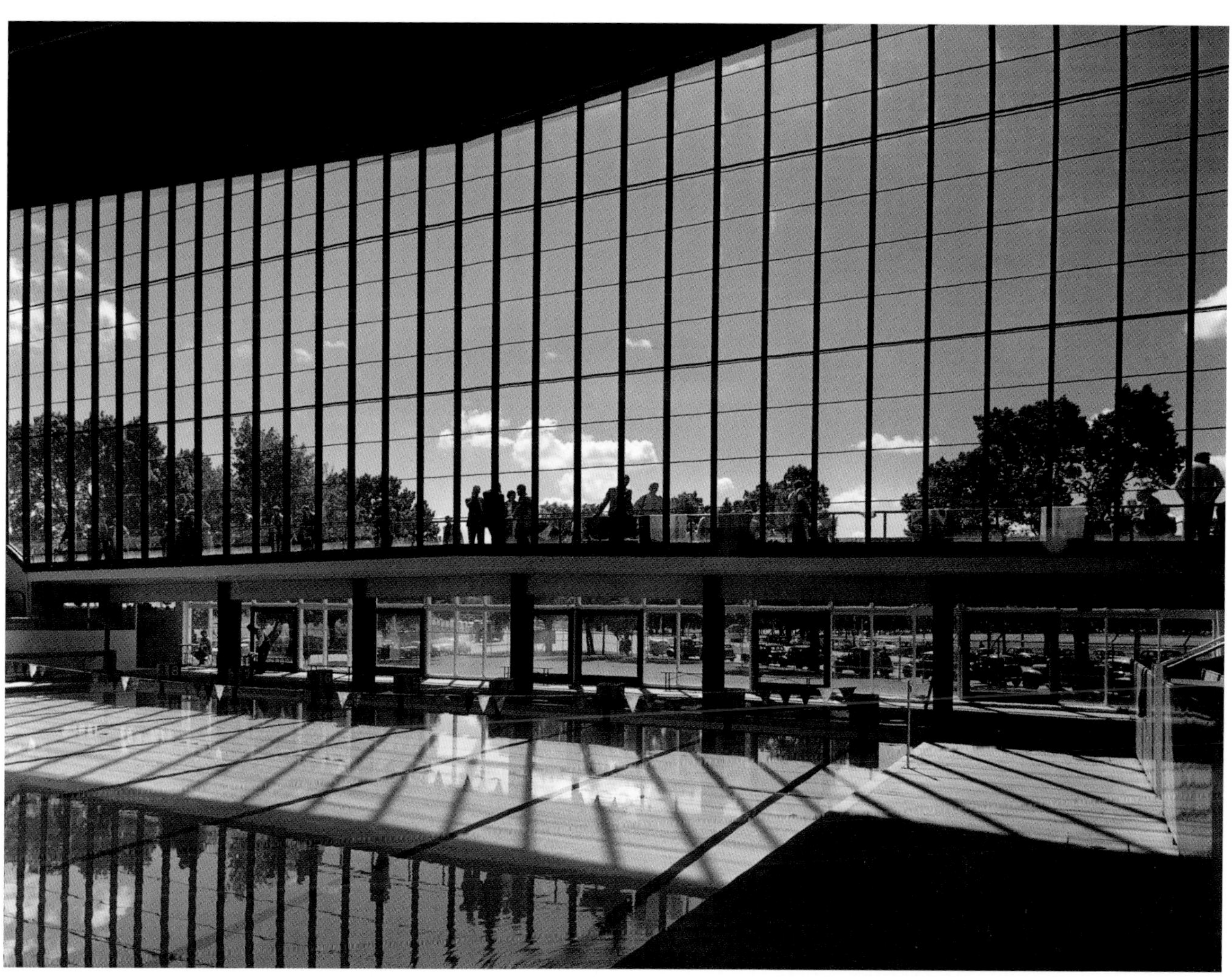

Olympic Swimming Pool, Melbourne, Victoria 1956
gelatin silver photograph; 48.4 × 37.8cm
nla.cat-vn2588867

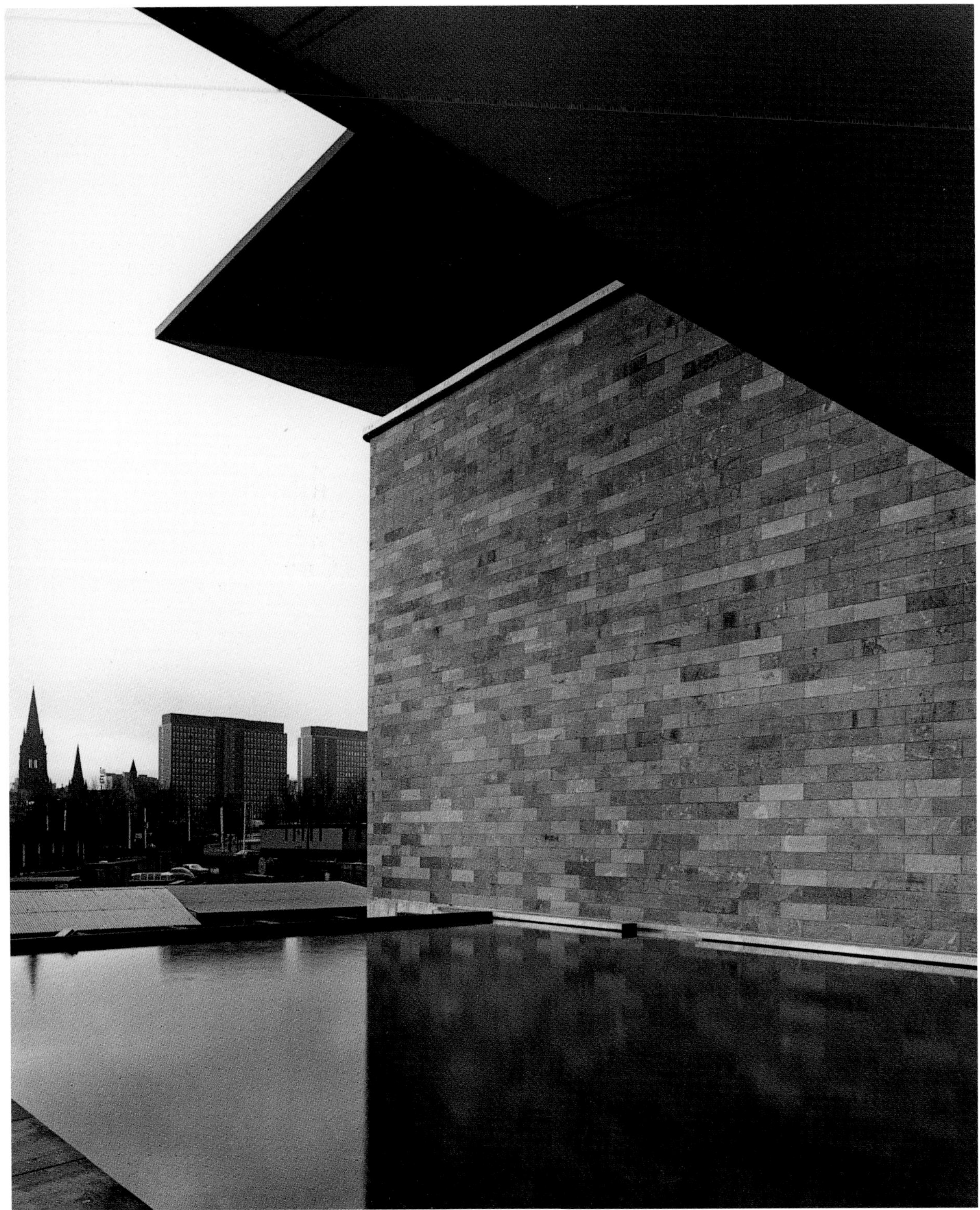

Comalco Aluminium Used in the Construction of the National Gallery of Victoria, Melbourne, Architect Roy Grounds 1968 [18]
gelatin silver photograph; 24.6 × 19.8cm
nla.cat-vn4306828

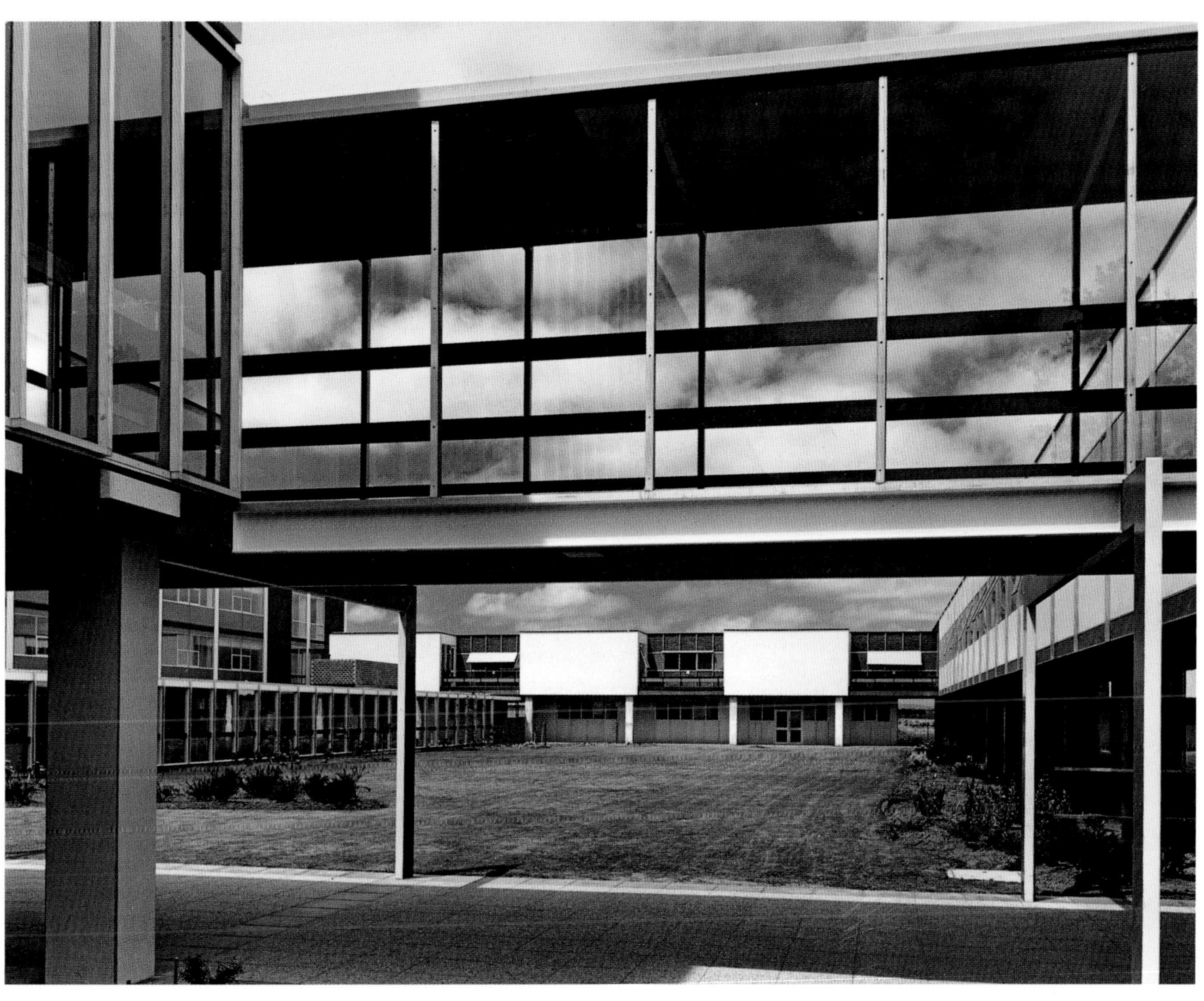

Engineering Buildings at Monash University, Clayton, Victoria, Architects Bates, Smart and McCutcheon 1962
gelatin silver photograph; 19.7 × 24.2cm
nla.cat-vn4192388

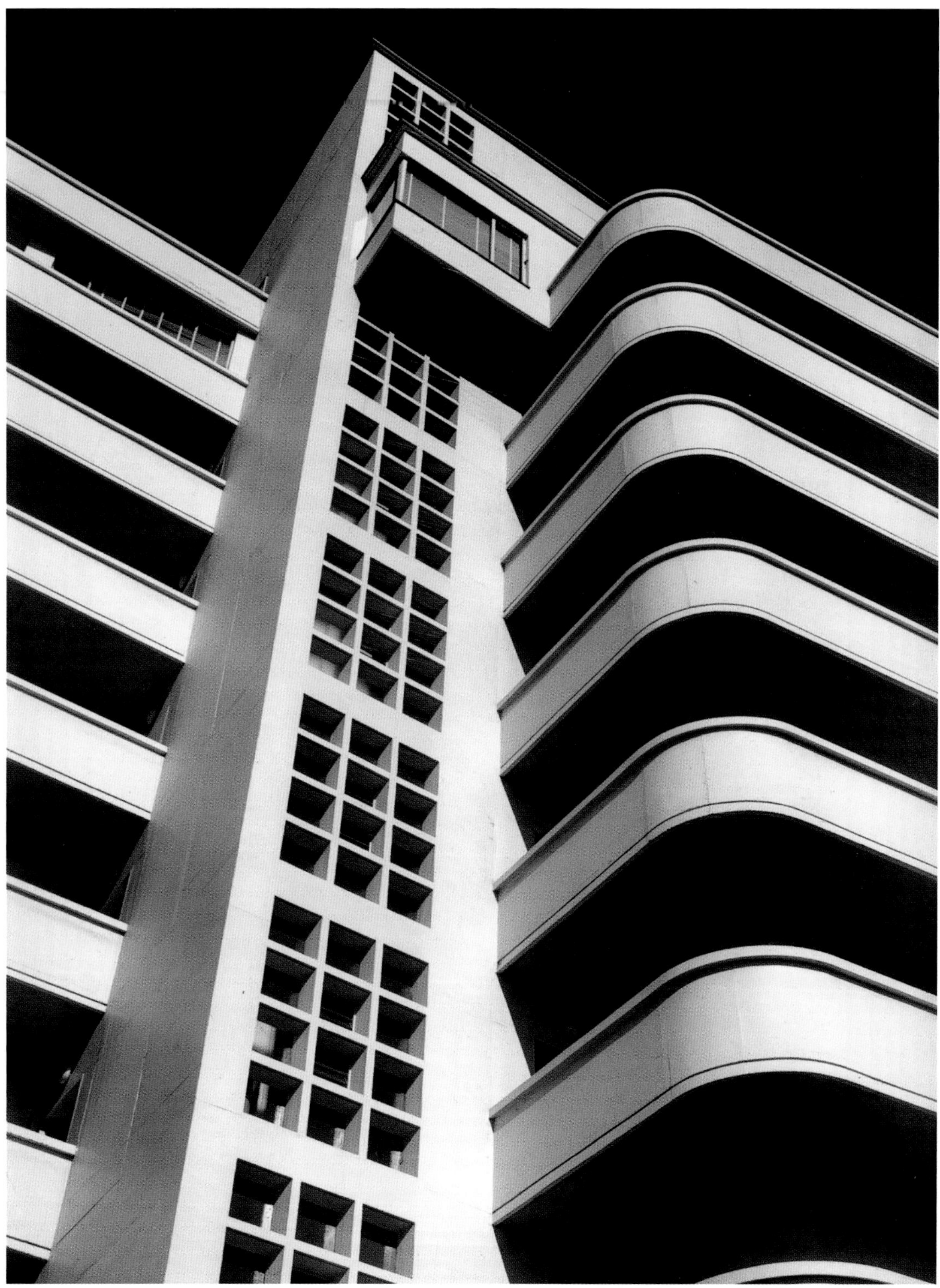

'Stanhill', Designed by Architect Frederick Romberg, at Queens Road, Melbourne, Victoria 1951 [1]
gelatin silver photograph; 49.3 × 35.9cm
nla.cat-vn719735

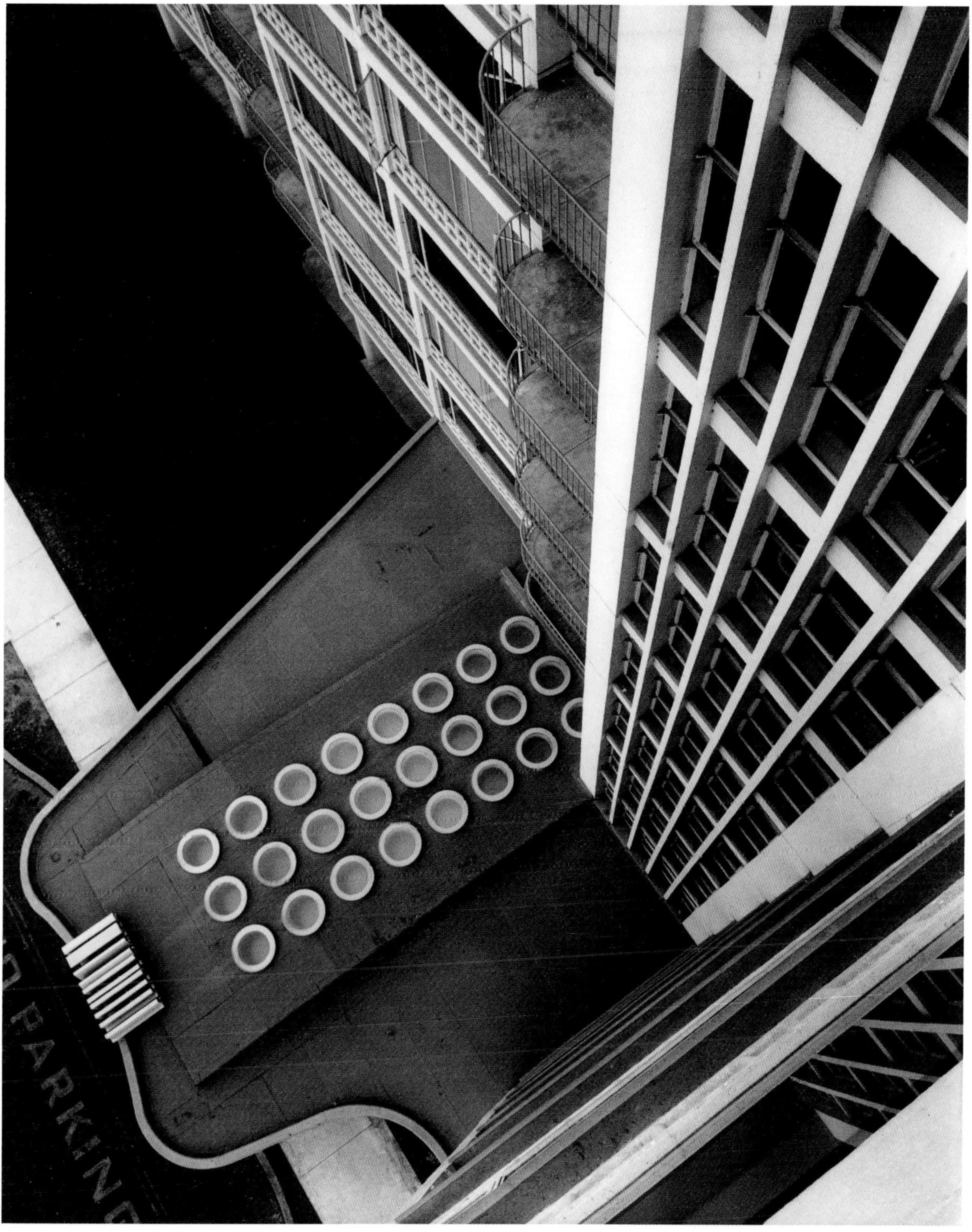

'Stanhill', Designed by Architect Frederick Romberg, at Queens Road, Melbourne, Victoria 1951 [2]
gelatin silver photograph; 50.1 × 39.5cm
nla.cat-vn719872

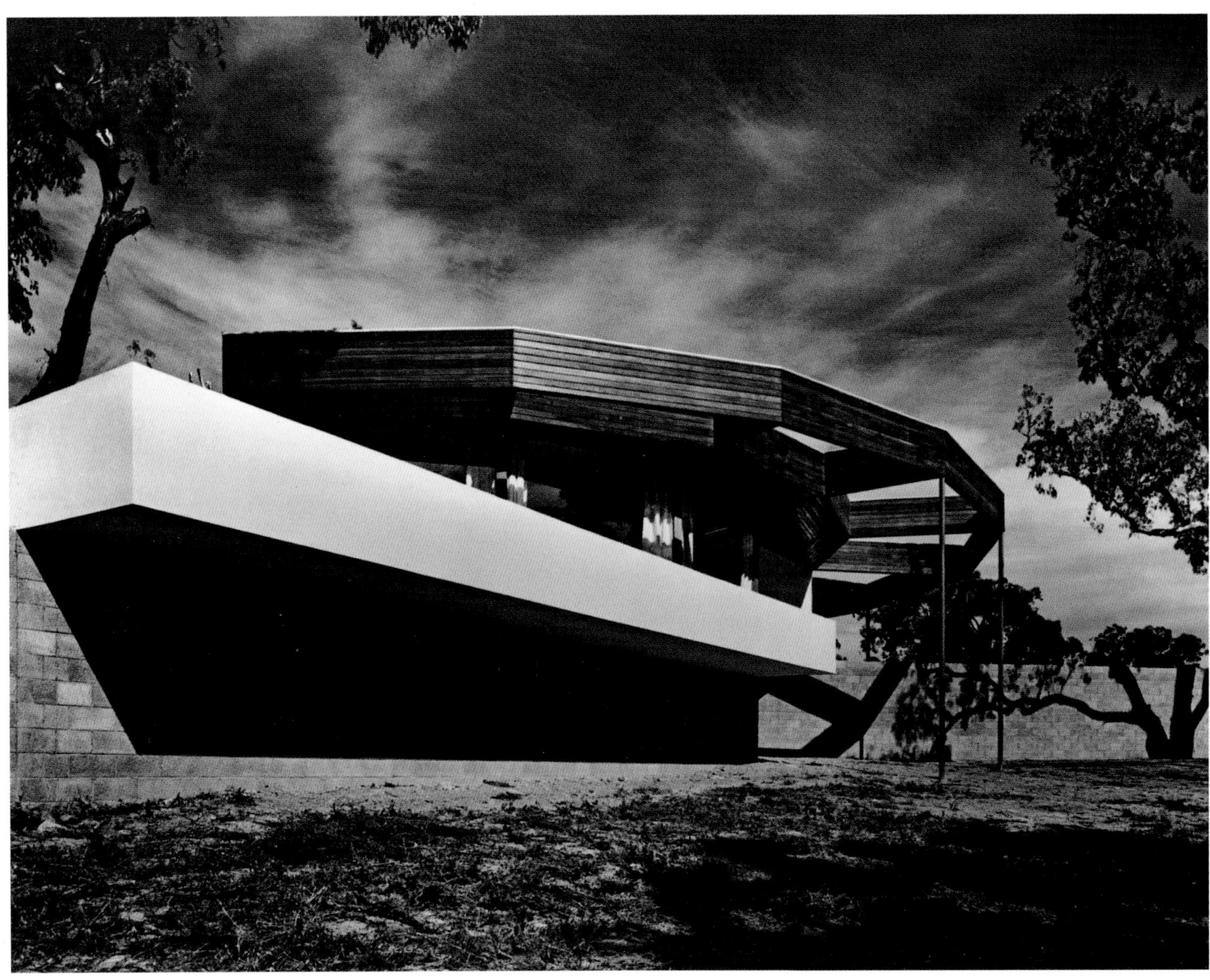

House of Professor Benjamin, Deakin, Australian Capital Territory 1958
gelatin silver photograph; 20 × 25cm
nla.cat-vn2266476

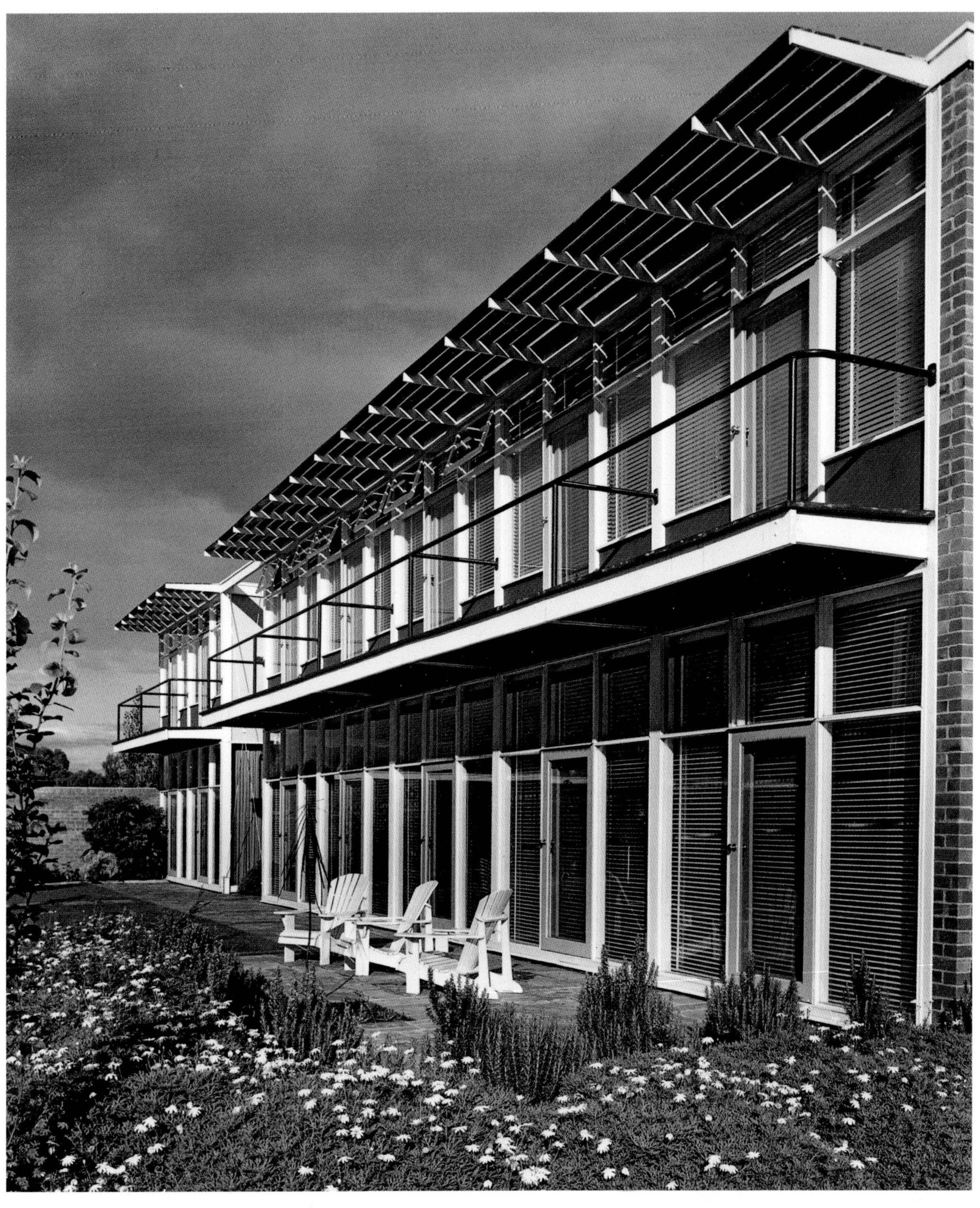

Bruck Mills Guest House, Wangaratta, Victoria, Architect Robyn Boyd 1956
gelatin silver photograph; 24 × 19.3cm
nla.cat-vn4087648

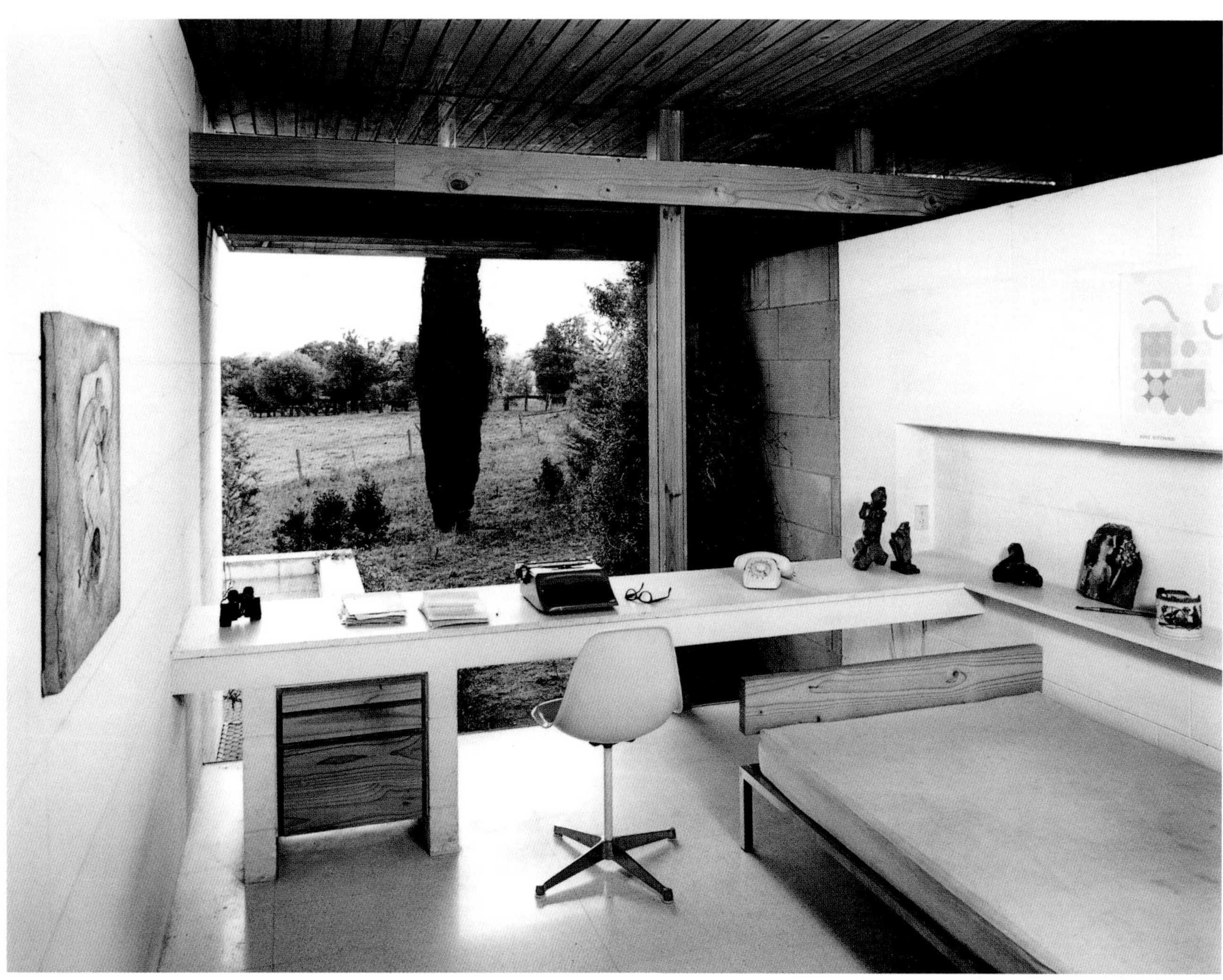

John Reed's Study at 'Heide', Templestowe, Victoria, Architect David McGlashan 1968
gelatin silver photograph; 19.2 × 24.2cm
nla.cat-vn3313008

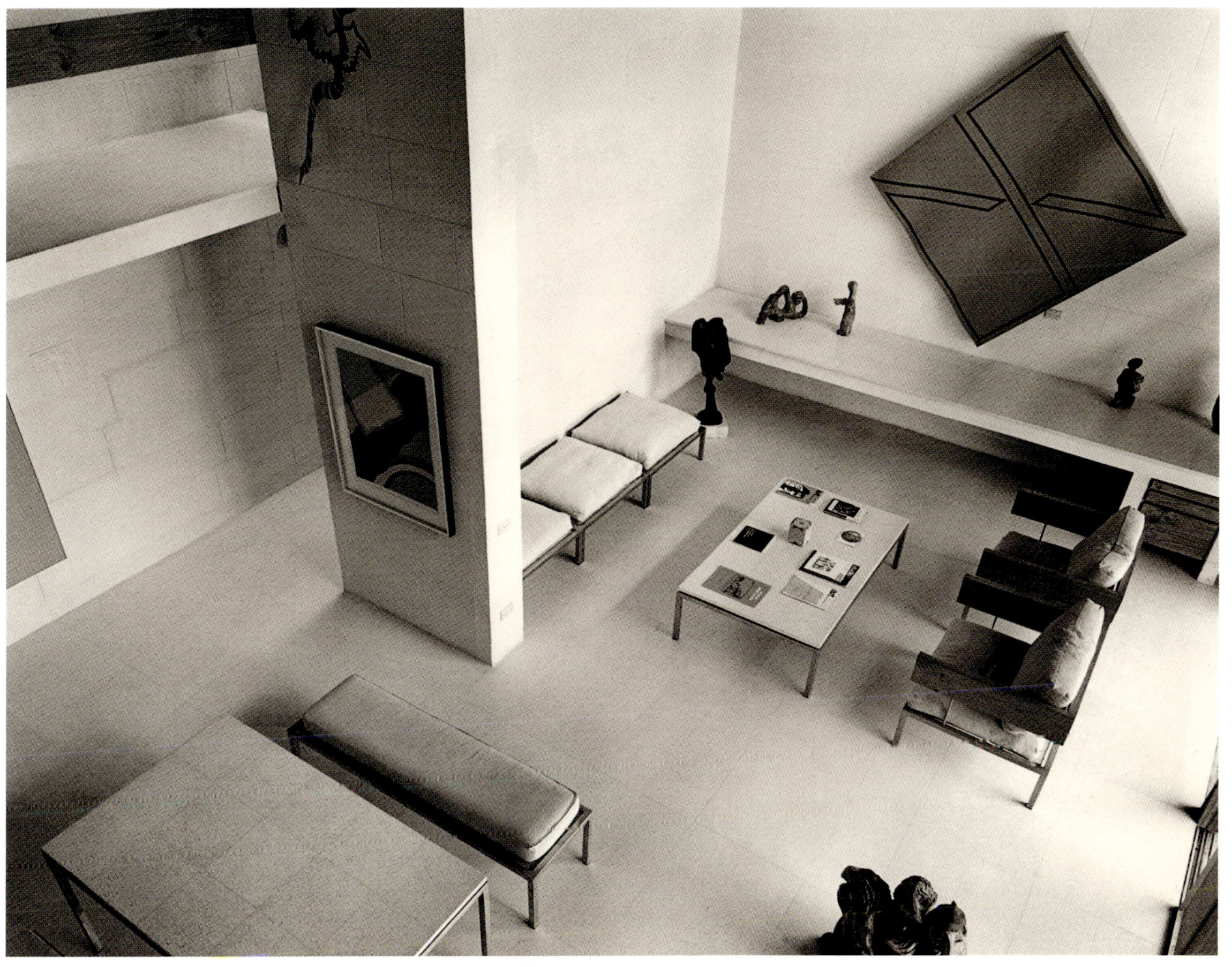

Interior of 'Heide', John and Sunday Reed's House in Templestowe, Victoria 1968
gelatin silver photograph; 19.3 × 24.5cm
nla.cat-vn4559174

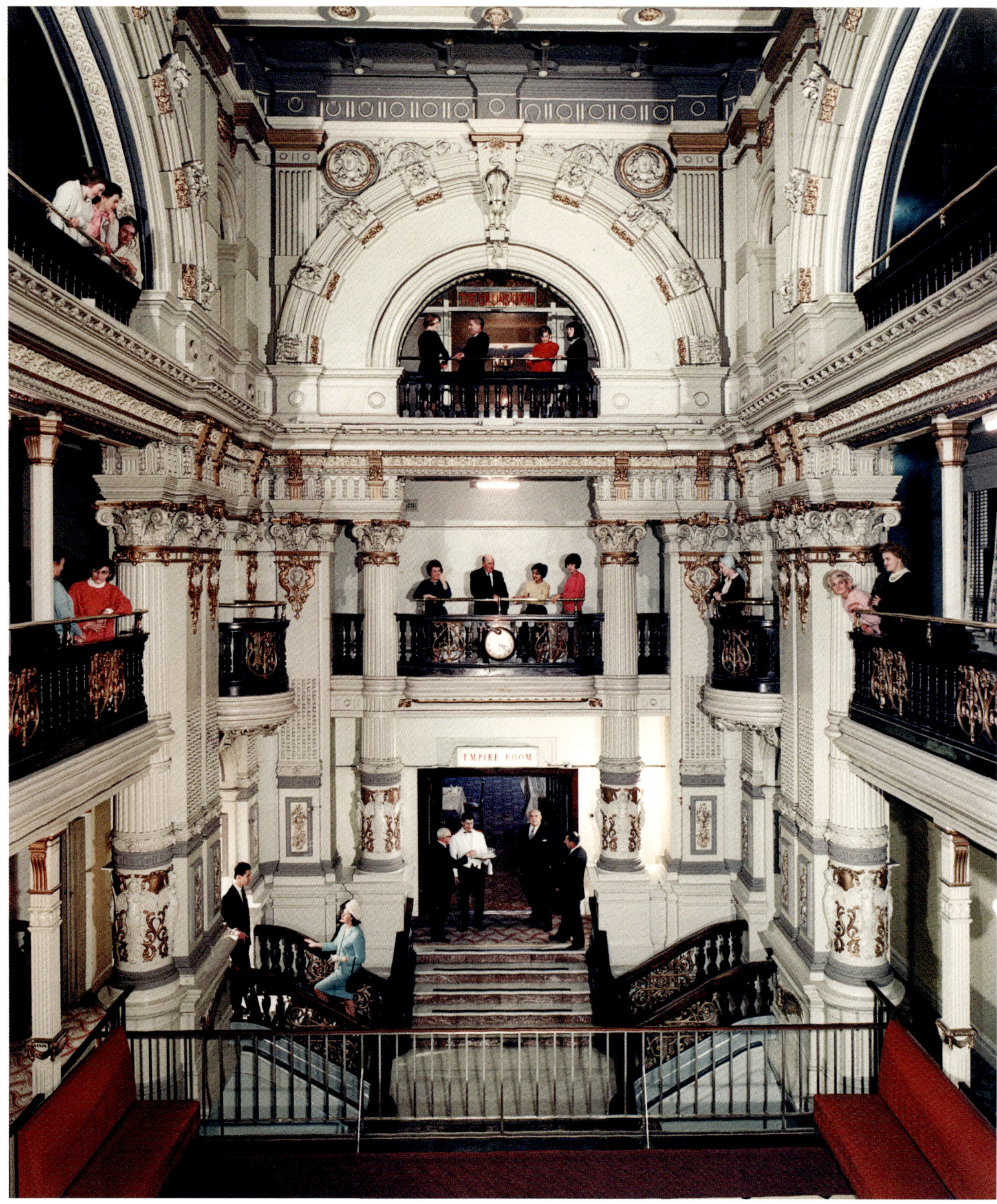

Federal Hotel, South West Corner Collins and King Streets, Melbourne, Victoria 1965
type C photograph; 38.5 × 49cm
nla.cat-vn2515806

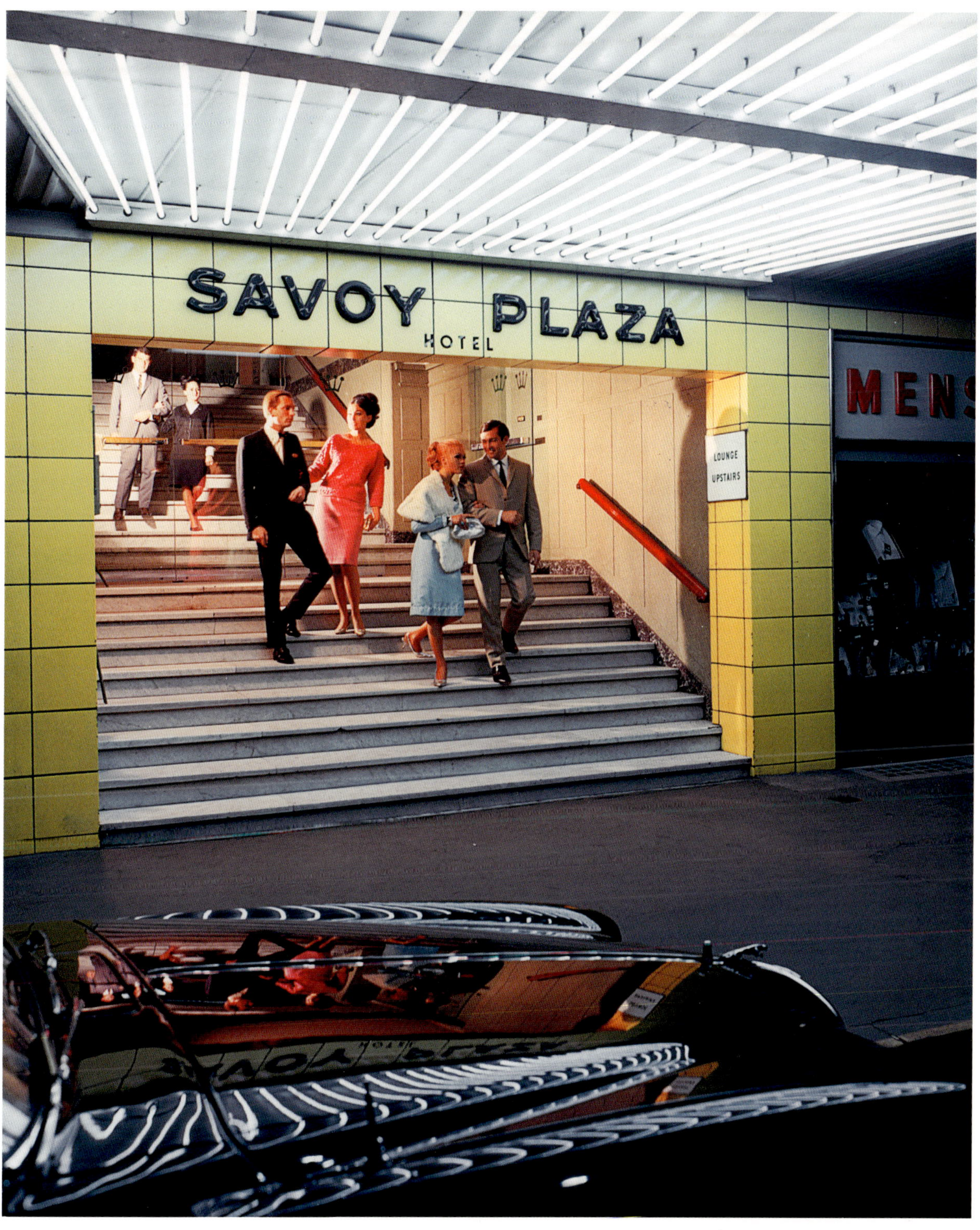

[People Walking Down the Front Steps of the] Savoy Plaza Hotel, Spencer Street, Melbourne, Victoria 1965
type C photograph; 25.3 × 20.2cm
nla.cat-vn3413235

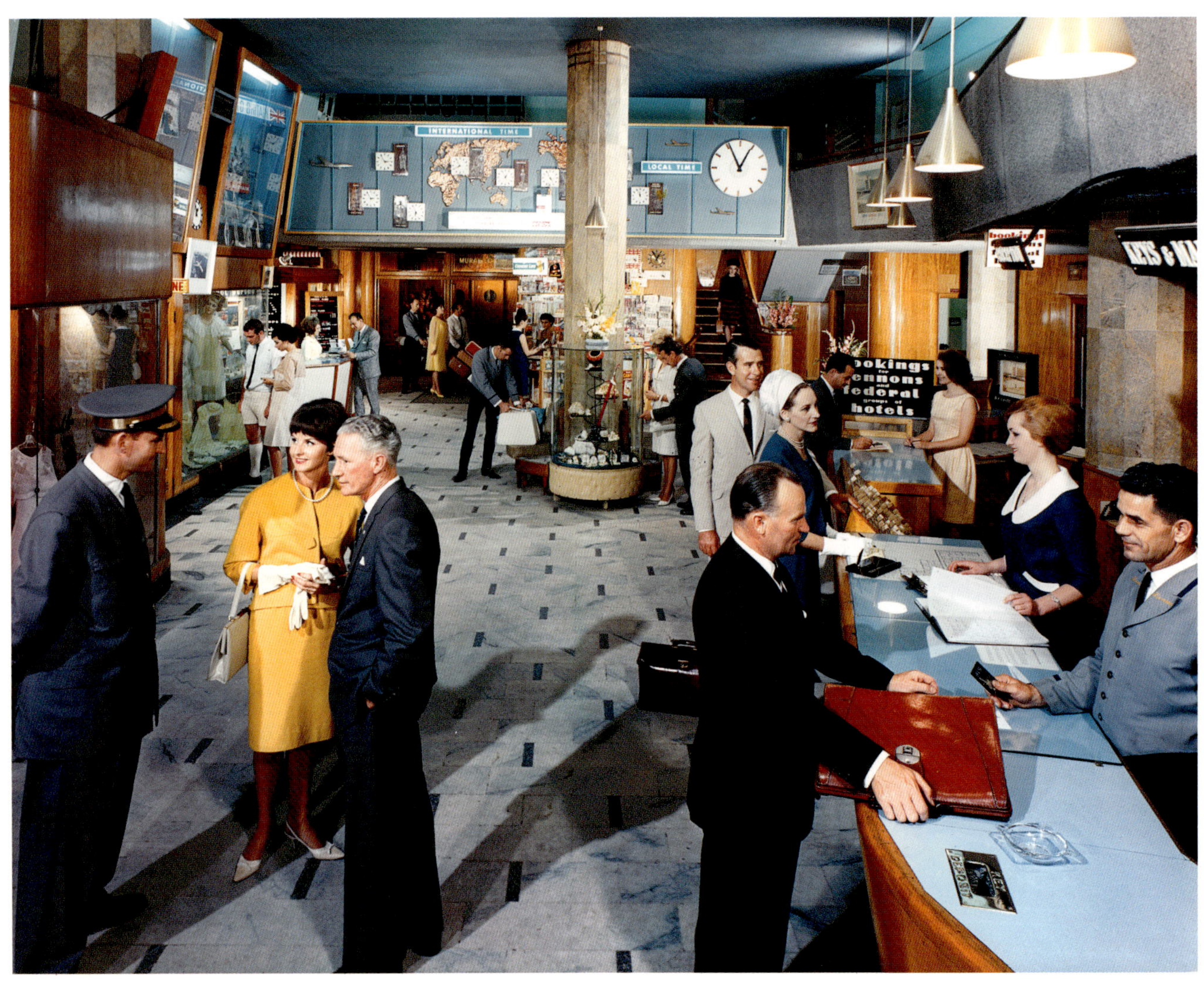

[Reception Area of] Lennons Hotel, Brisbane, Queensland 1965
type C photograph; 20.6 × 25.4cm
nla.cat-vn3311445

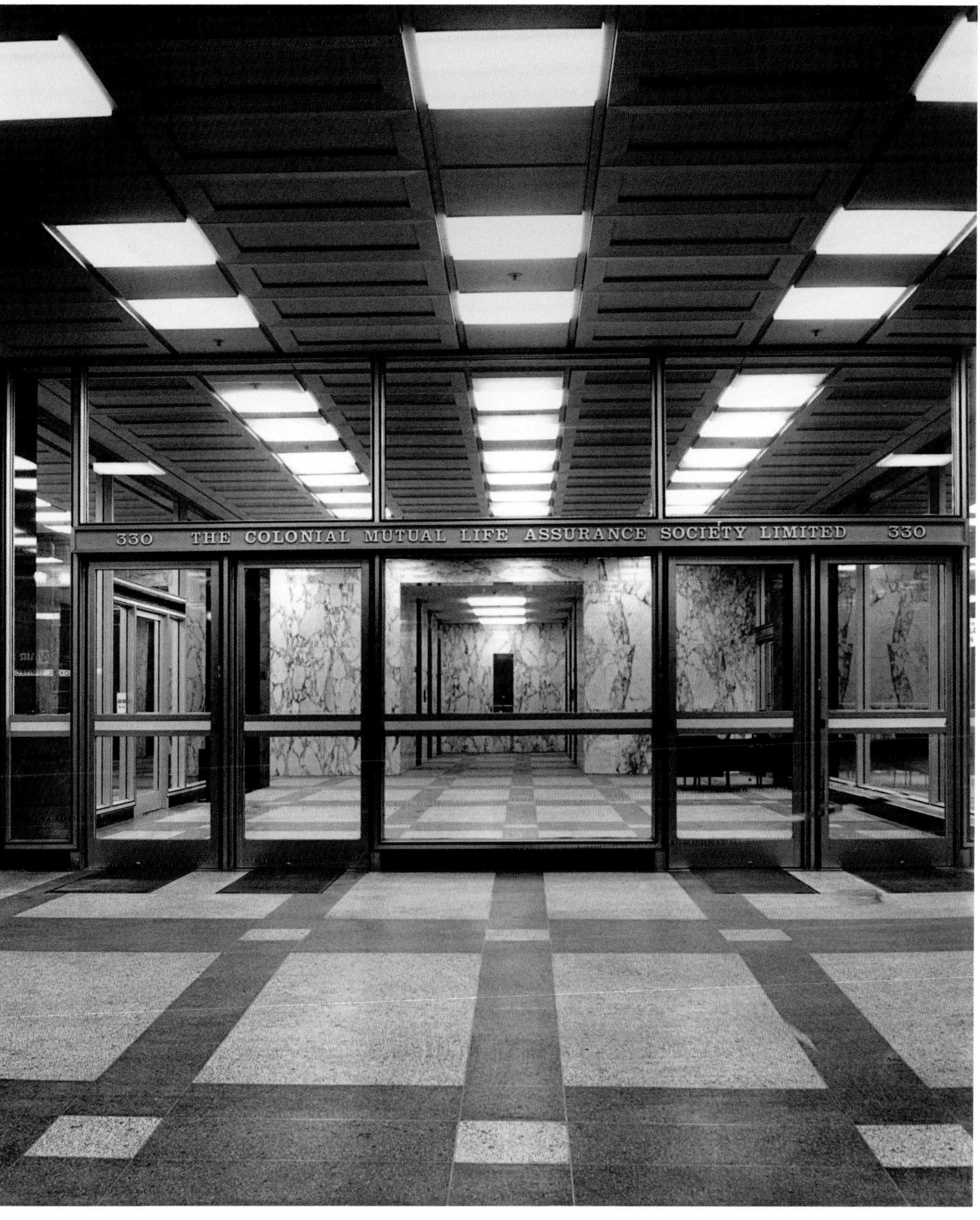

[Entrance to] the New Colonial Mutual Life Building, Corner of Collins and Elizabeth Streets, Melbourne, Victoria 1963
gelatin silver photograph; 24.4 × 19.4cm
nla.cat-vn3267625

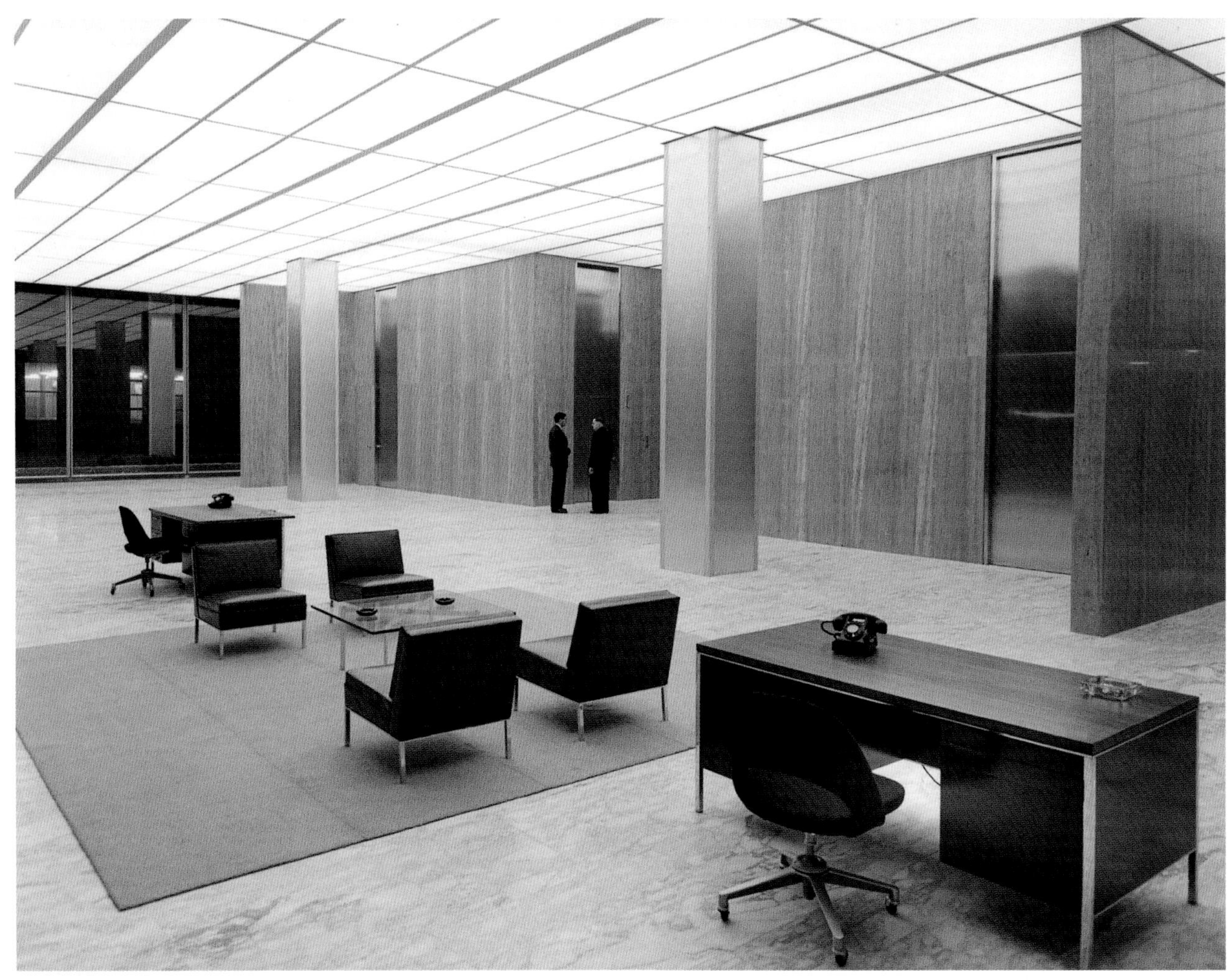

Shell House, Bourke and Williams Streets, Melbourne, Victoria, Architects Buchan, Laird & Buchan 1960
gelatin silver photograph; 19.4 × 24.4cm
nla.cat-vn3085907

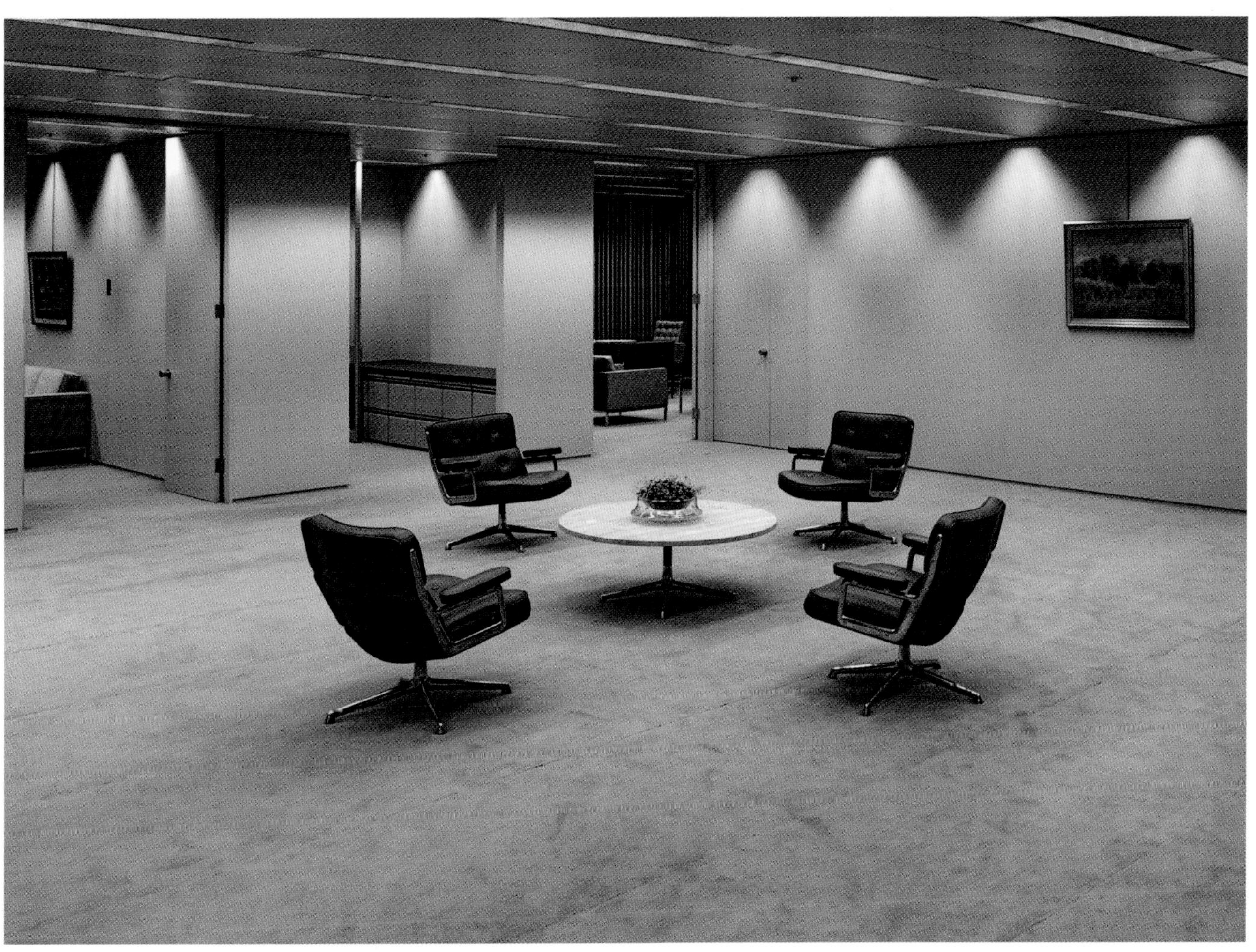

[A Meeting Area in the Offices of the] Eagle Star Building, Bourke Street, Melbourne, Victoria, Architects Yuncken Freeman 1972
gelatin silver photograph; 18.8 × 25cm
nla.cat-vn3486756

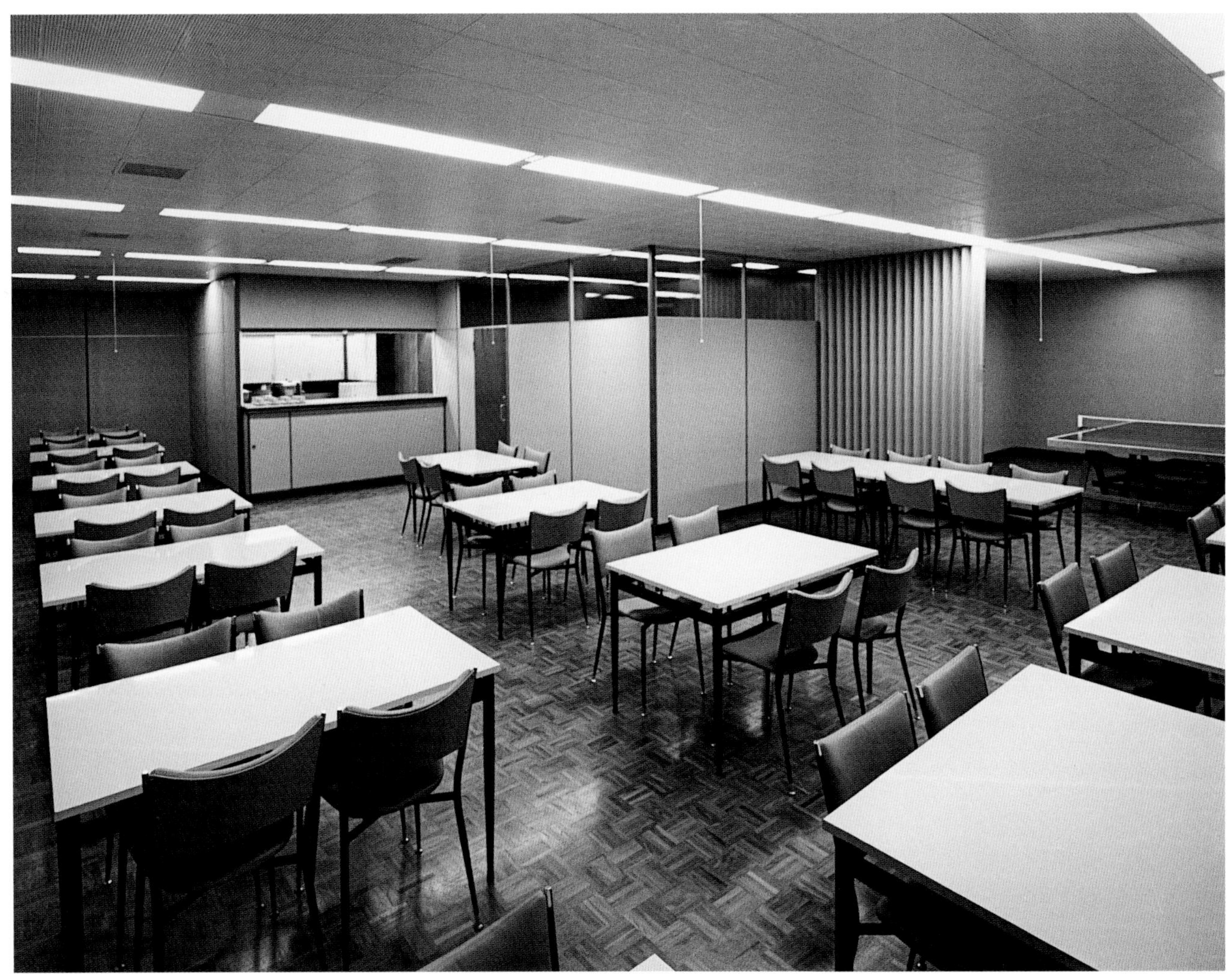

Amenities Room, New Zealand Insurance Company Building, Bourke Street, Melbourne, Victoria, Architects Bates, Smart and McCutcheon 1961
gelatin silver photograph; 19.8 × 24.5cm
nla.cat-vn3971245

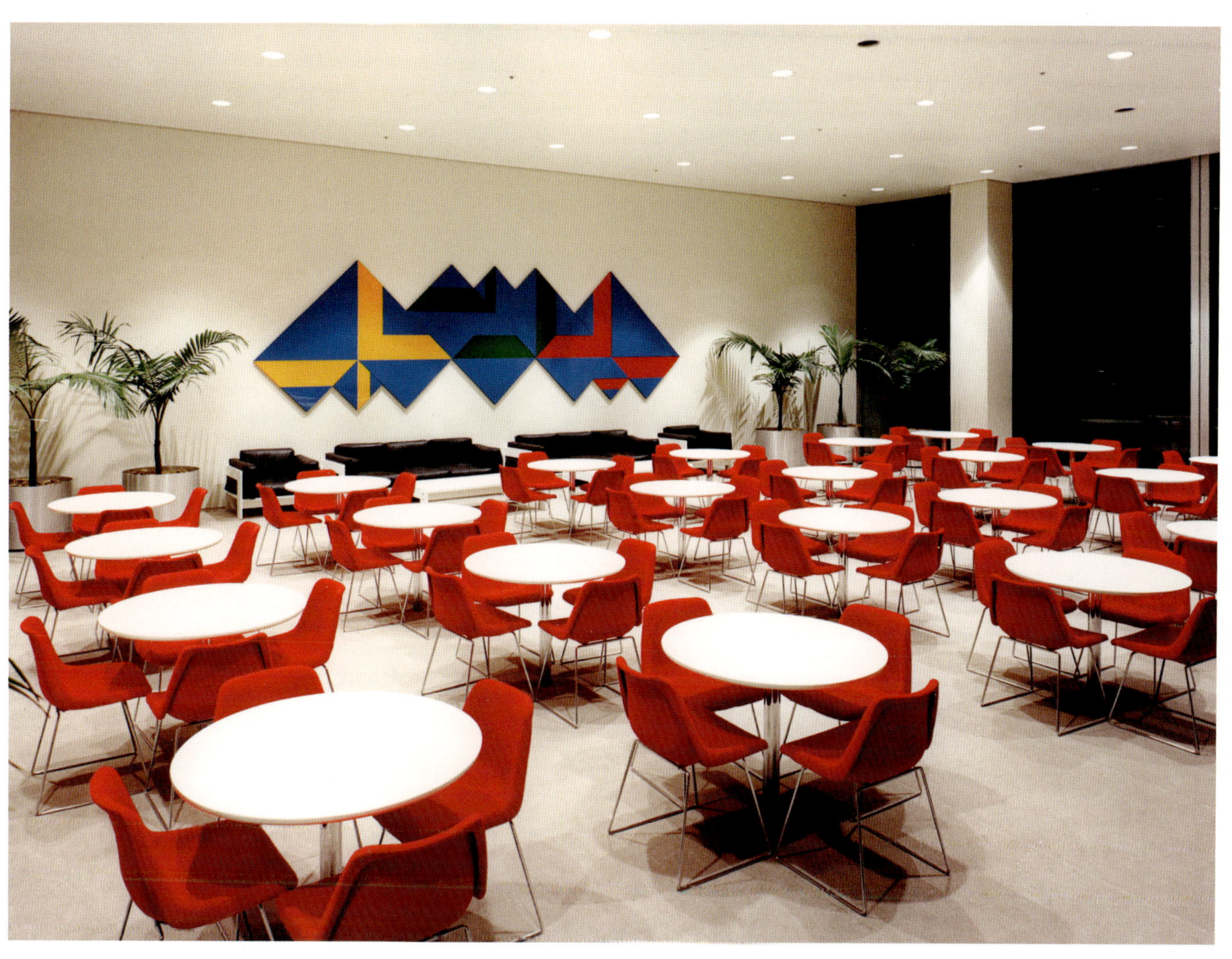

[Tables and Chairs in the Offices of the] Eagle Star Building, Bourke Street, Melbourne, Victoria, Architects Yuncken Freeman 1972
type C photograph; 18.7 × 24.5cm
nla.cat-vn3504363

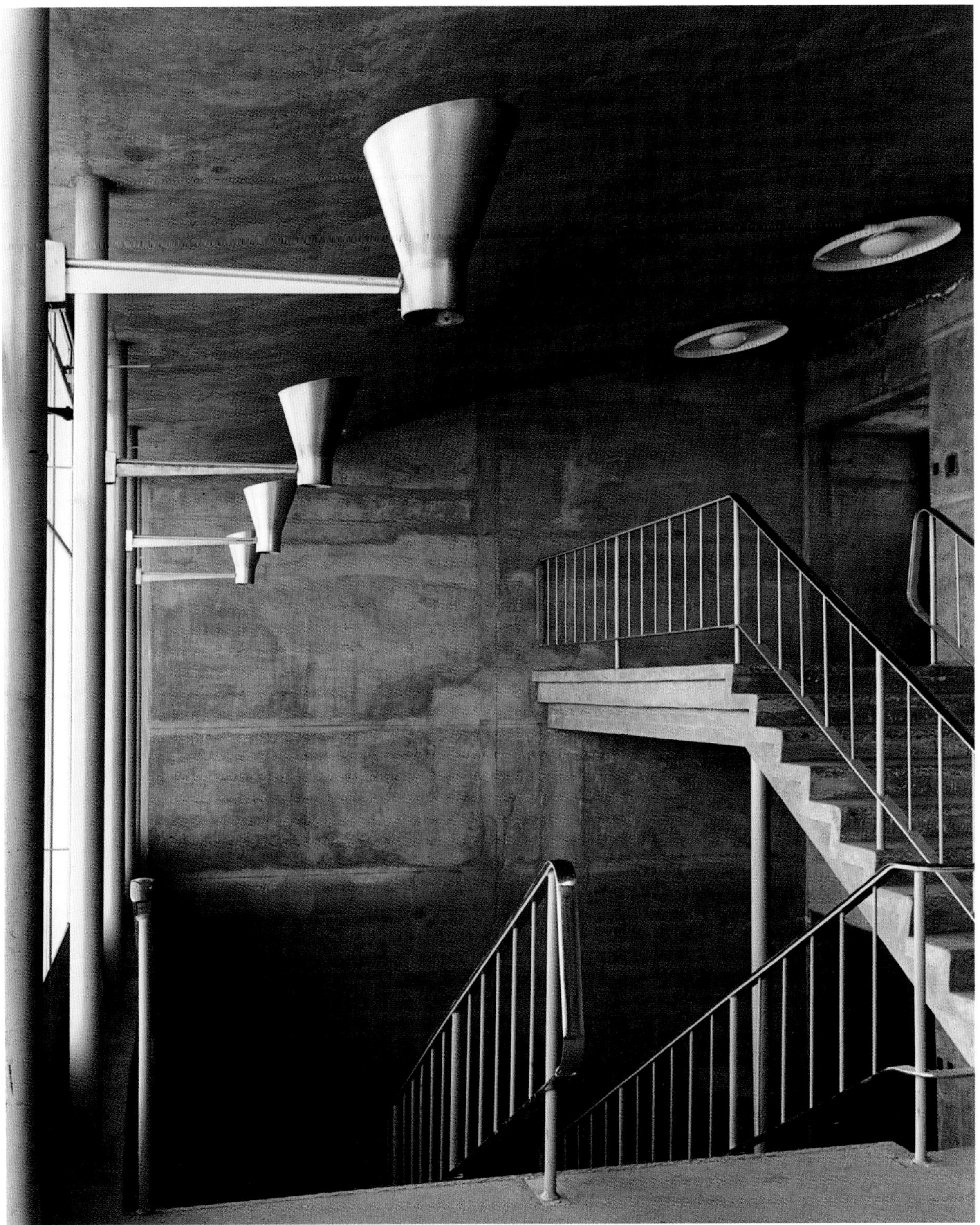

New Broken Hill Entrance to Administration Broken Hill, New South Wales 1959
gelatin silver photograph; 24.8 × 19.4cm
nla.cat-vn2591403

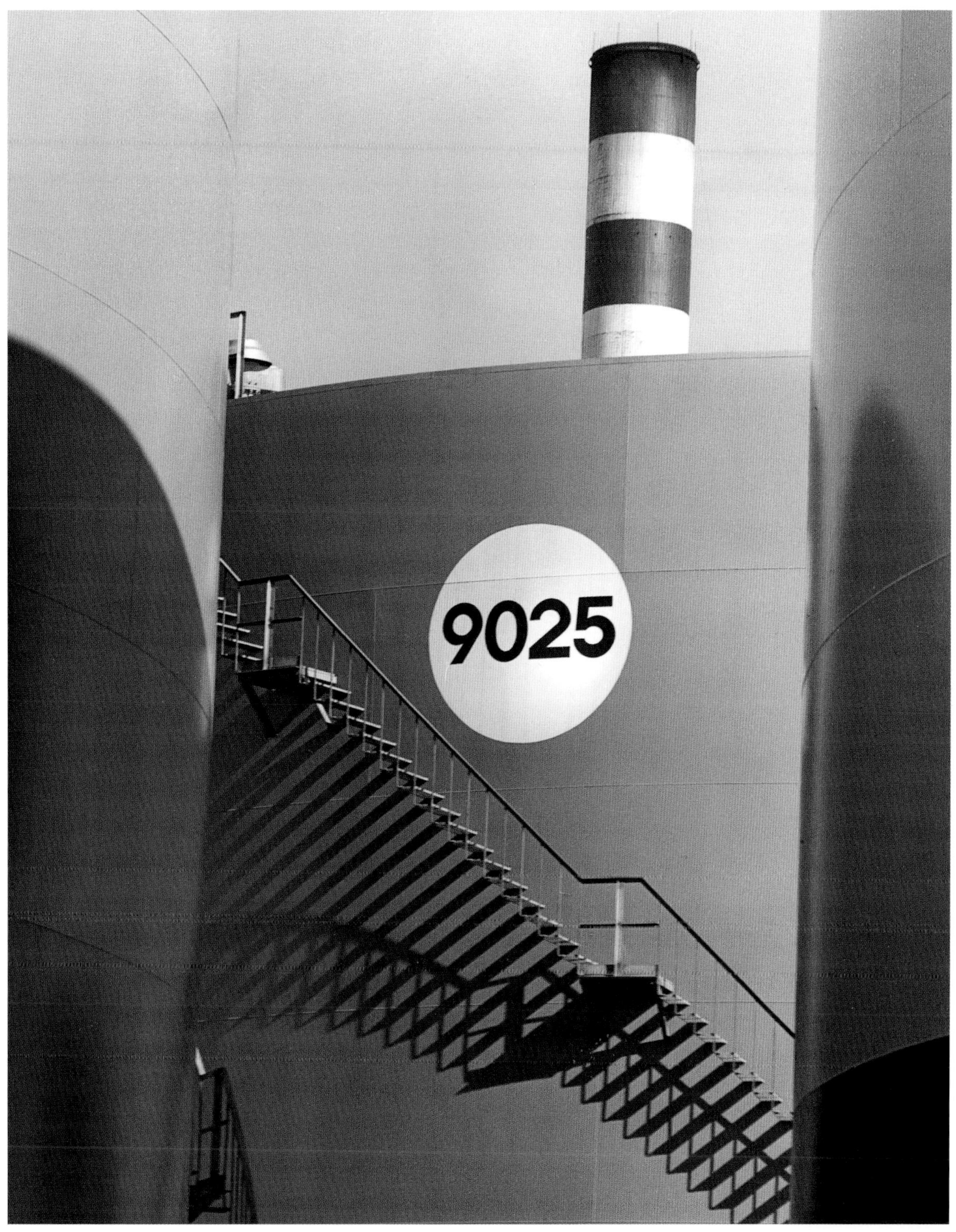

[Tank 9025], Mobil Oil Refinery, Port Stanvac, South Australia 1975
gelatin silver photograph; 25.3 × 19.7cm
nla.cat-vn3419328

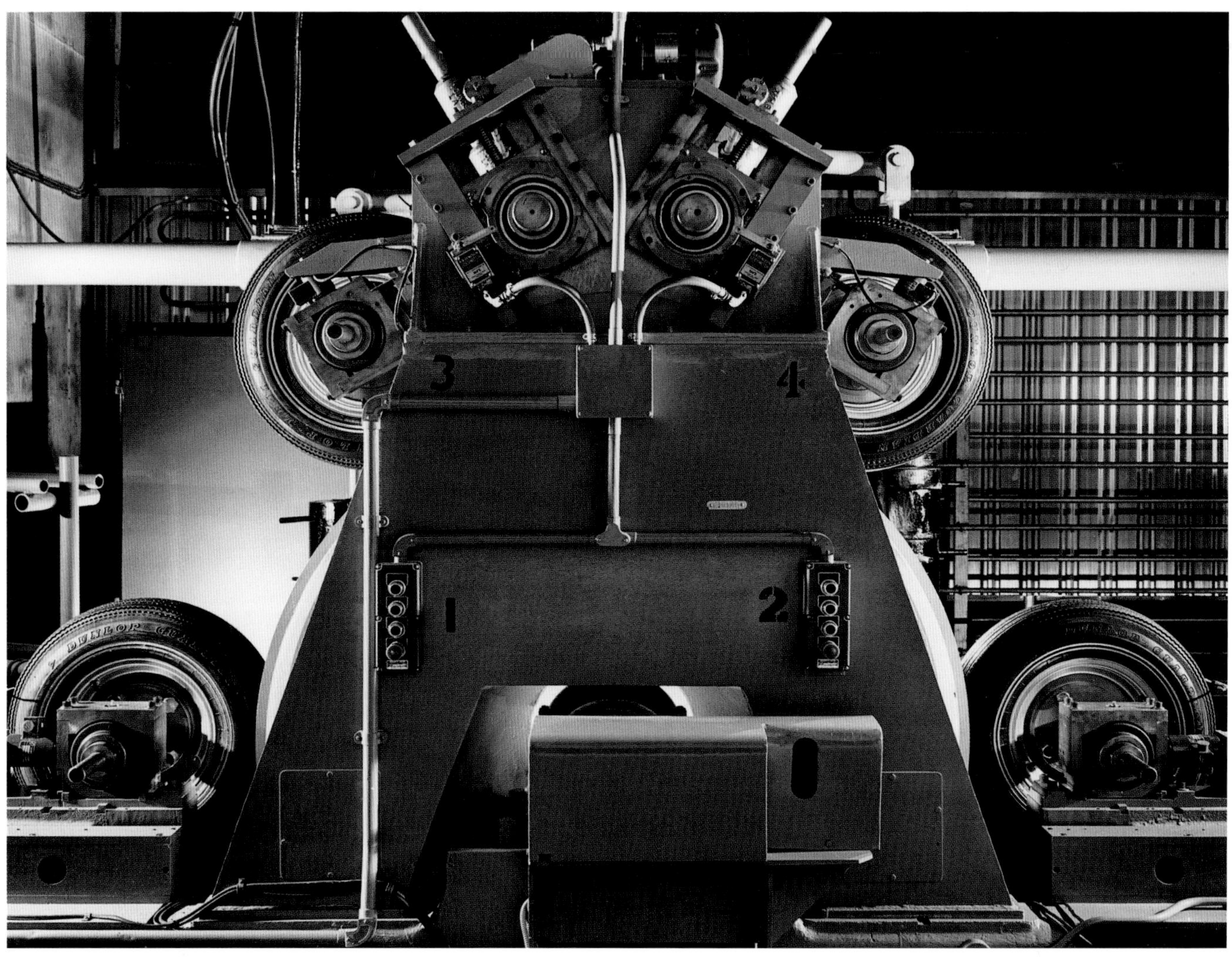

Dunlop Tyre Manufacturing, Bayswater, Victoria 1969
gelatin silver photograph; 19.3 × 24.8cm
nla.cat-vn3299069

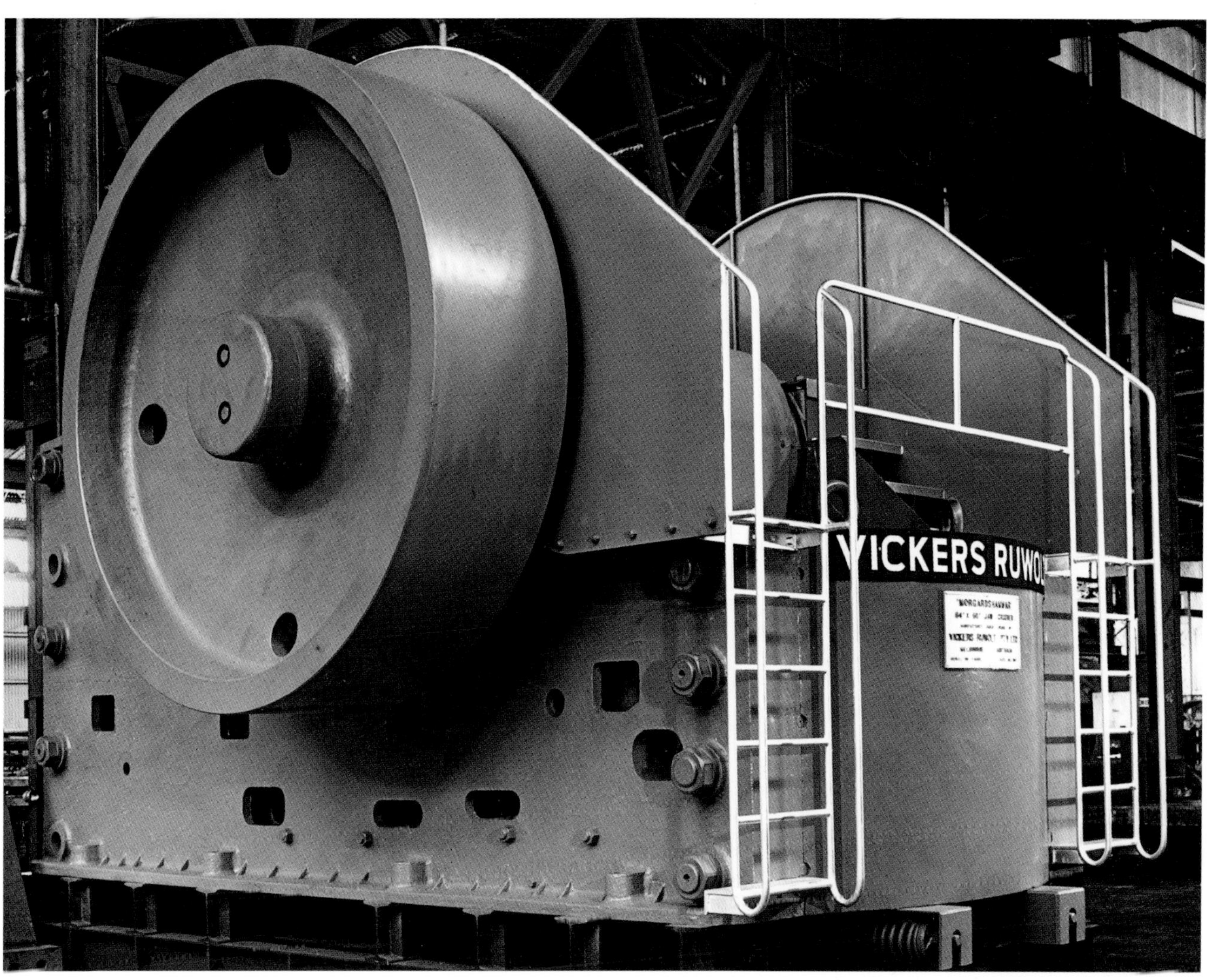

Morgards Hammer for Mining Industry, Vickers Ruwolt, Burnley, Victoria 1962
gelatin silver photograph; 19.8 × 24.6cm
nla.cat-vn3427897

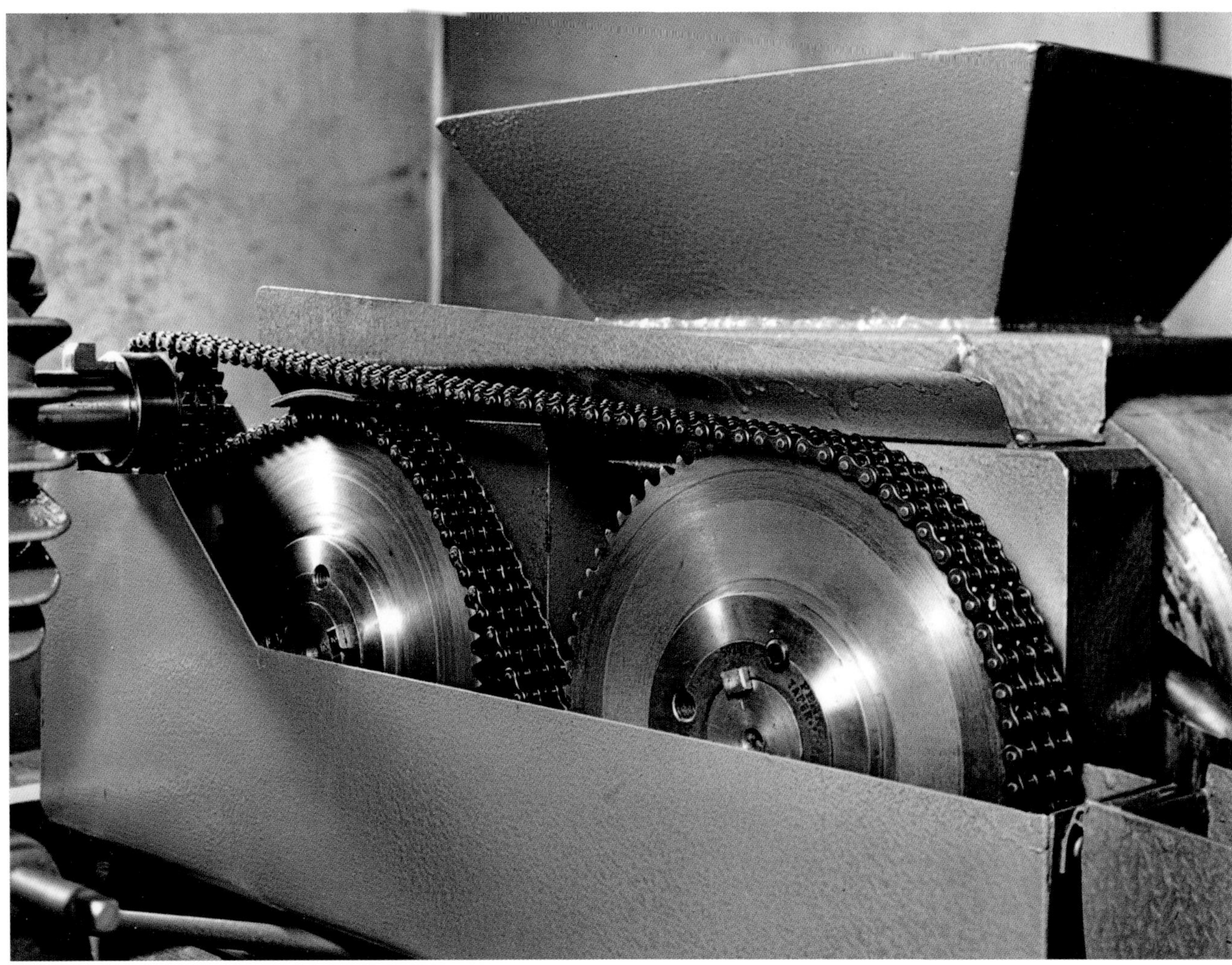

Laboratory Stone Crusher, Vickers Ruwolt, Burnley, Victoria 1968
gelatin silver photograph; 19.7 × 24.6cm
nla.cat-vn3428012

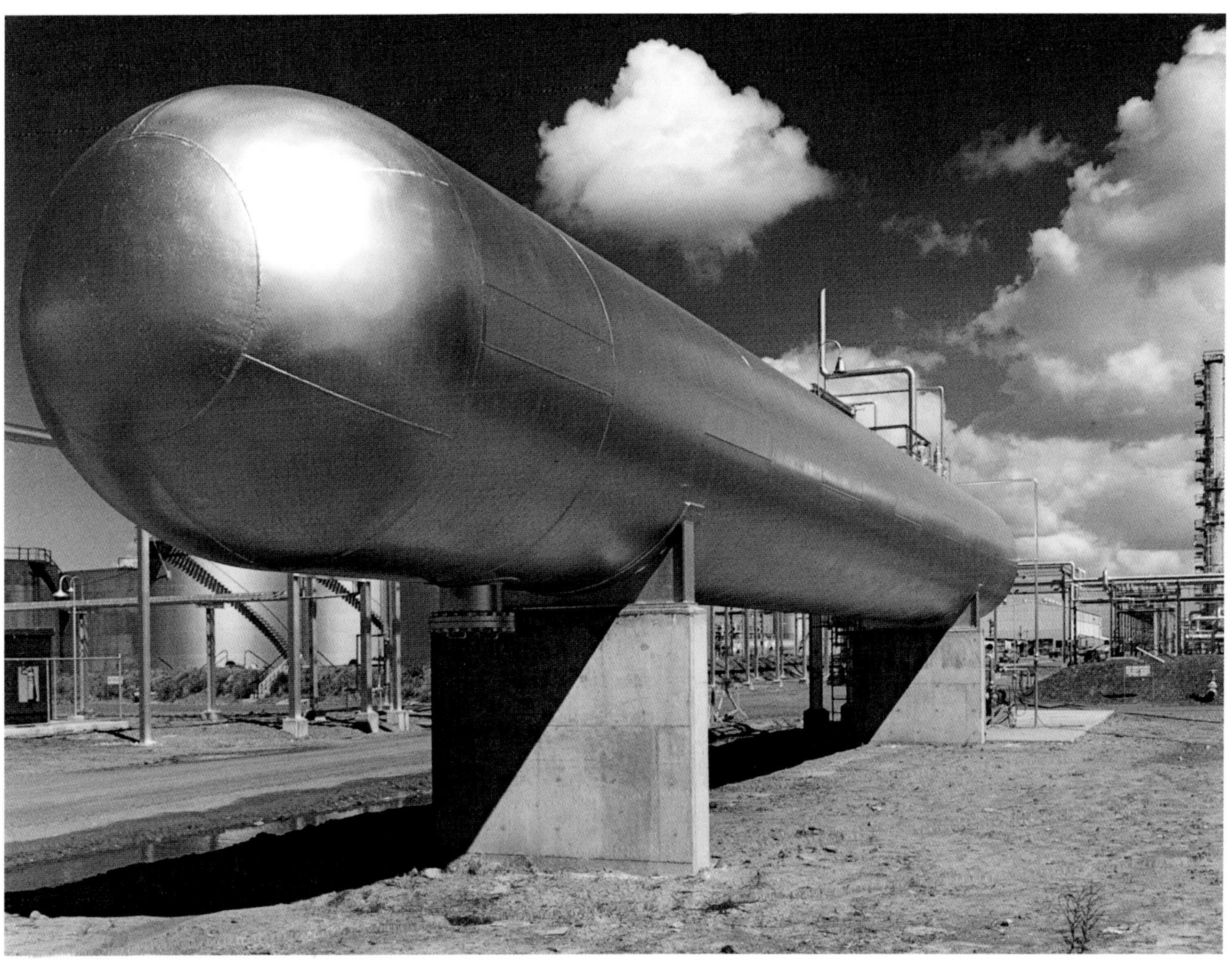

Large Storage Tank at Mobil's Stanvac Oil Refinery, Altona, Victoria 1956
gelatin silver photograph; 25.1 × 19.4cm
nla.cat-vn3419889

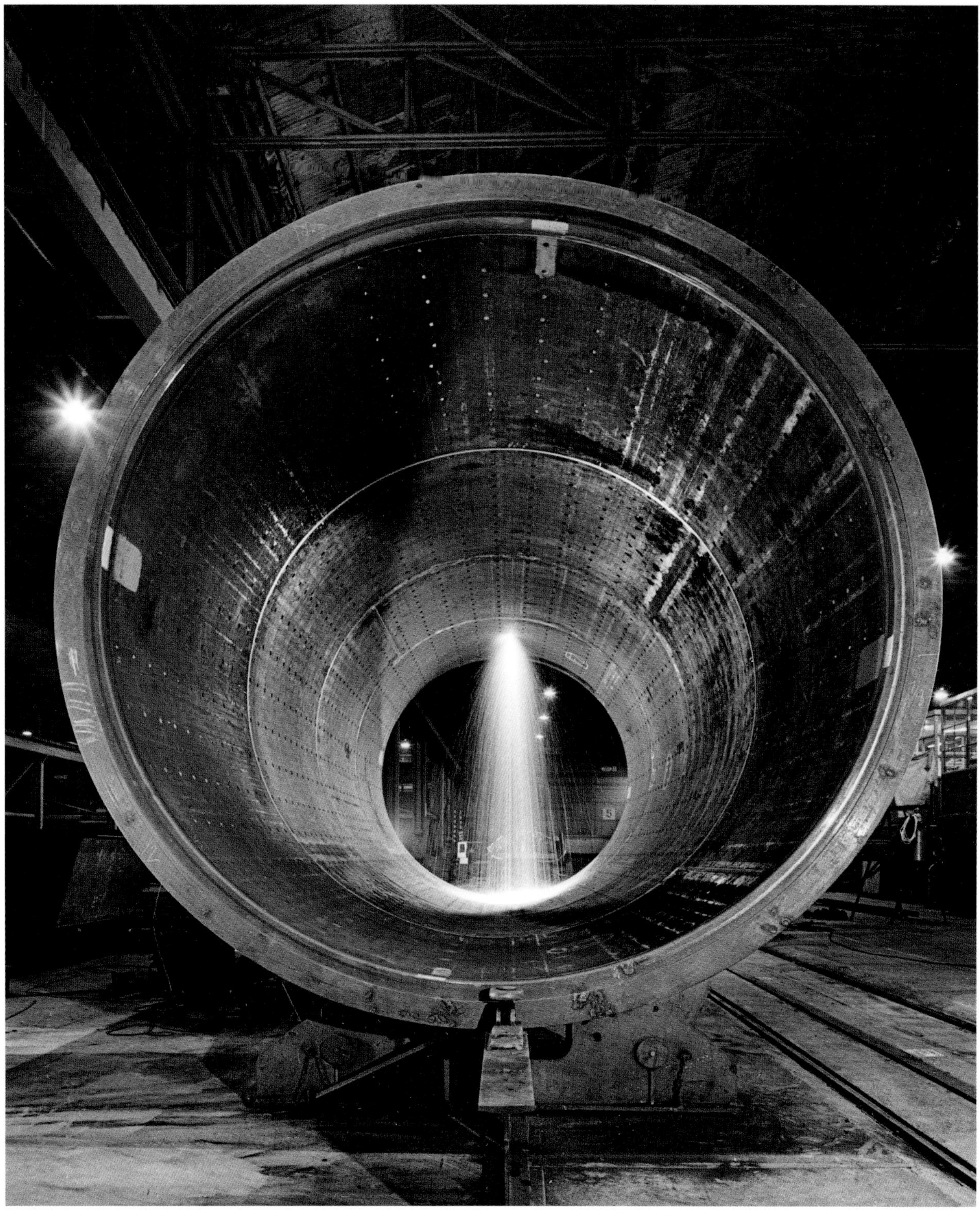

Vickers Ruwolt Rotary Cement Mill, Burnley, Victoria 1969
gelatin silver photograph; 24.4 × 19.8cm
nla.cat-vn3427934

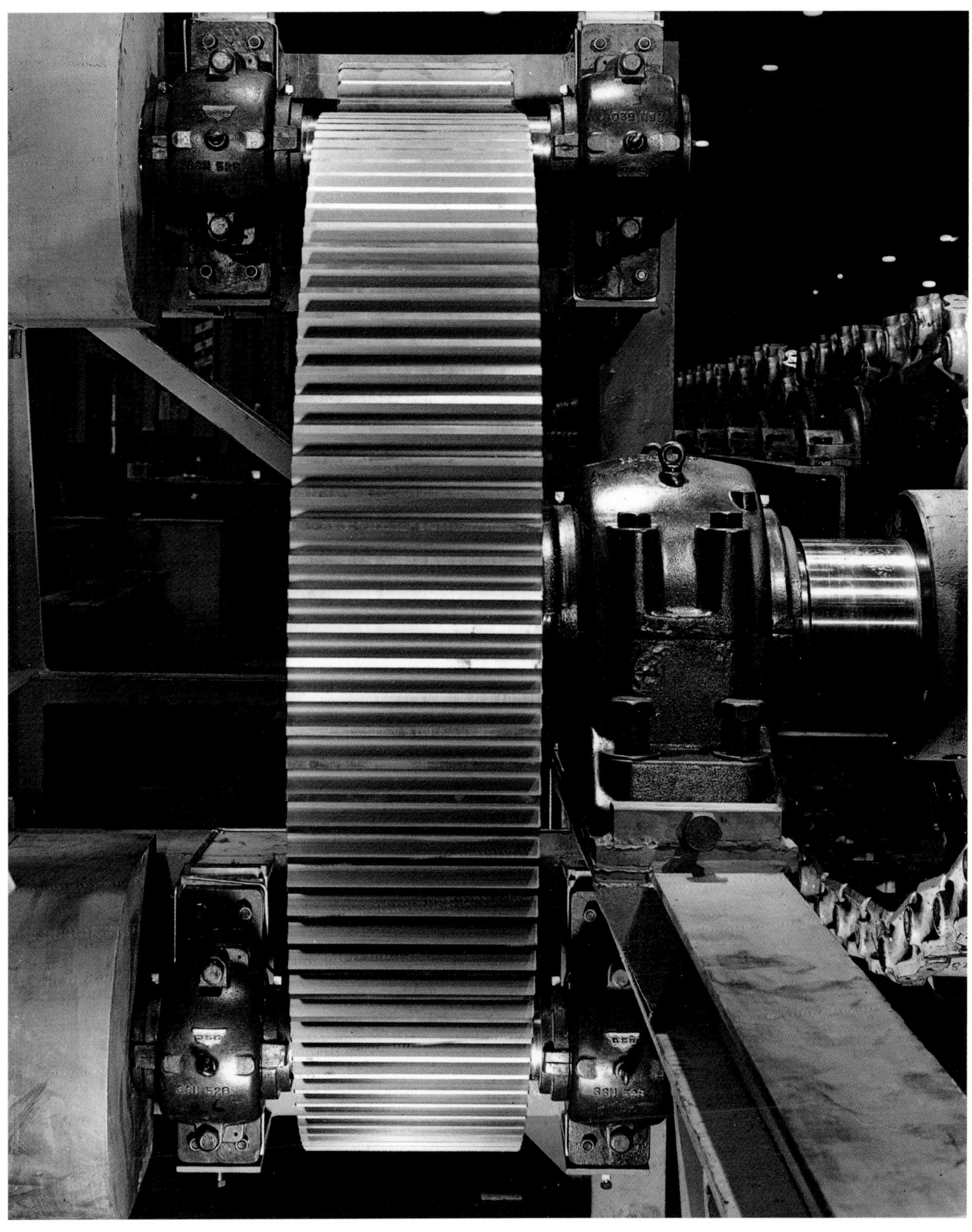

Gears and Housing by Vickers Ruwolt, Burnley, Victoria 1971
gelatin silver photograph; 19.6 × 24.9cm
nla.cat-vn3428810

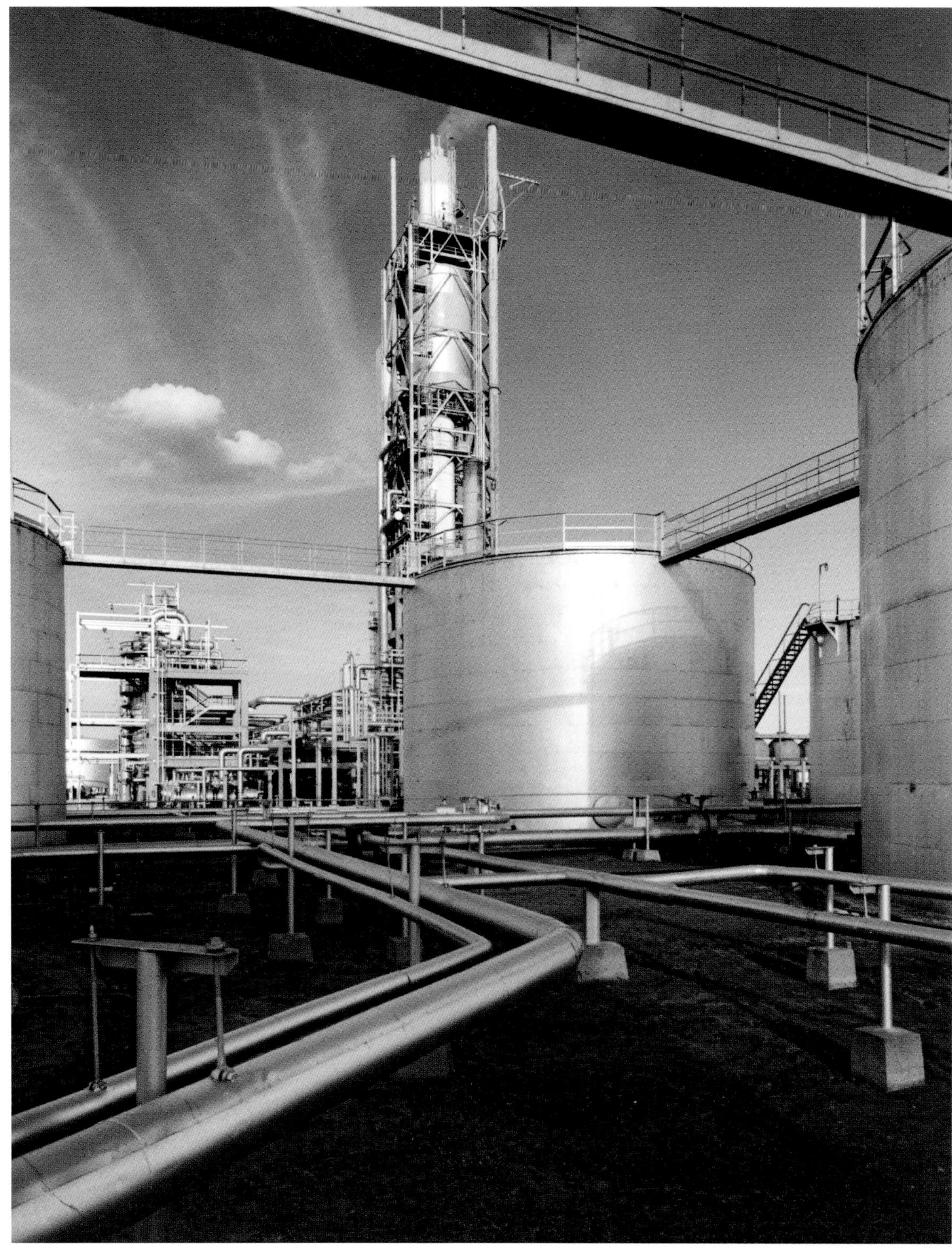

[Storage Tanks in Front of the Cracking Tower at the Mobil] Stanvac Oil Refinery, Altona, Victoria 1956
gelatin silver photograph; 24.2 × 18.3cm
nla.cat-vn3419822

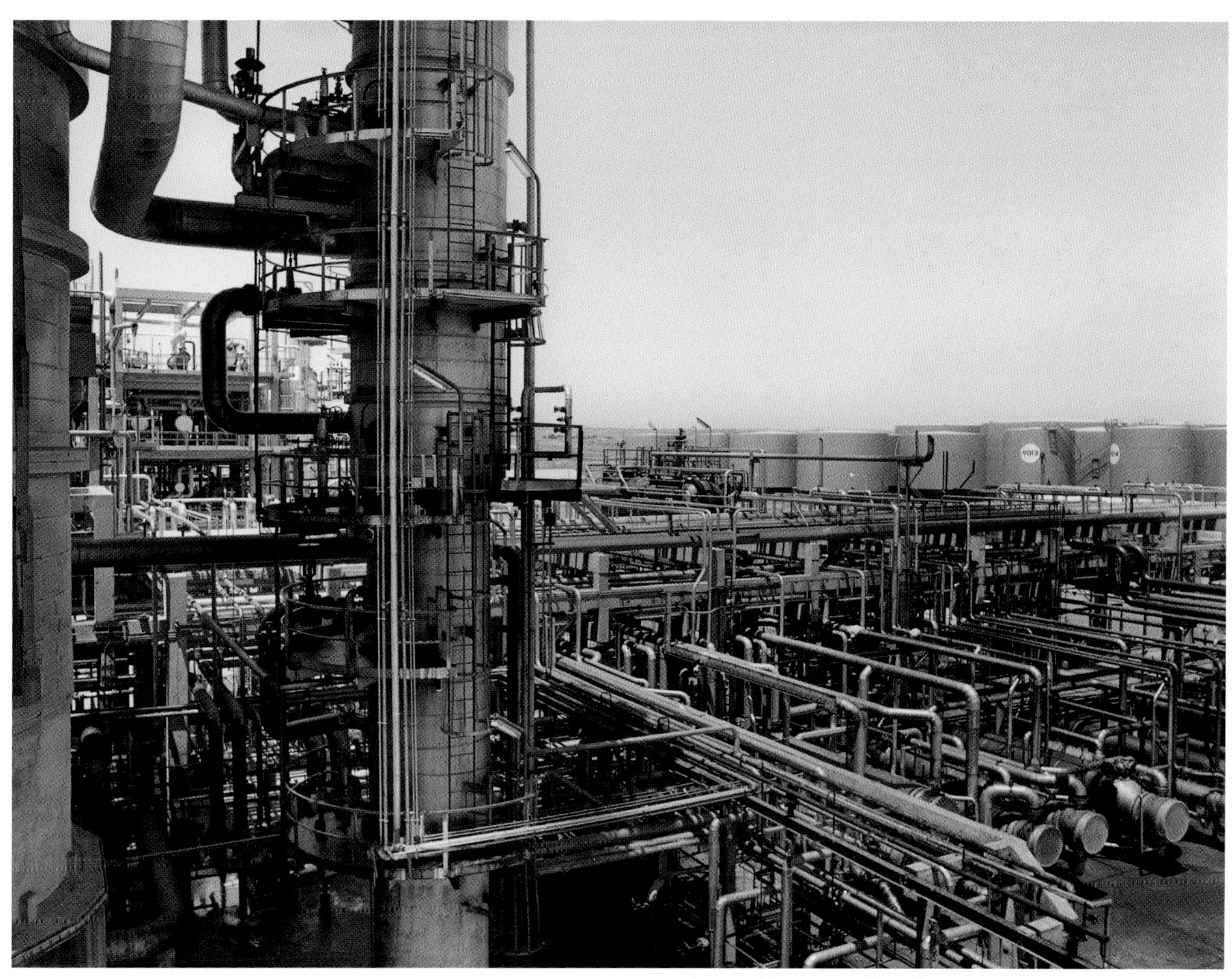

Mobil Lube Oil Refinery, Port Stanvac, South Australia 1975
gelatin silver photograph; 19.5 × 24.9cm
nla.cat-vn3419004

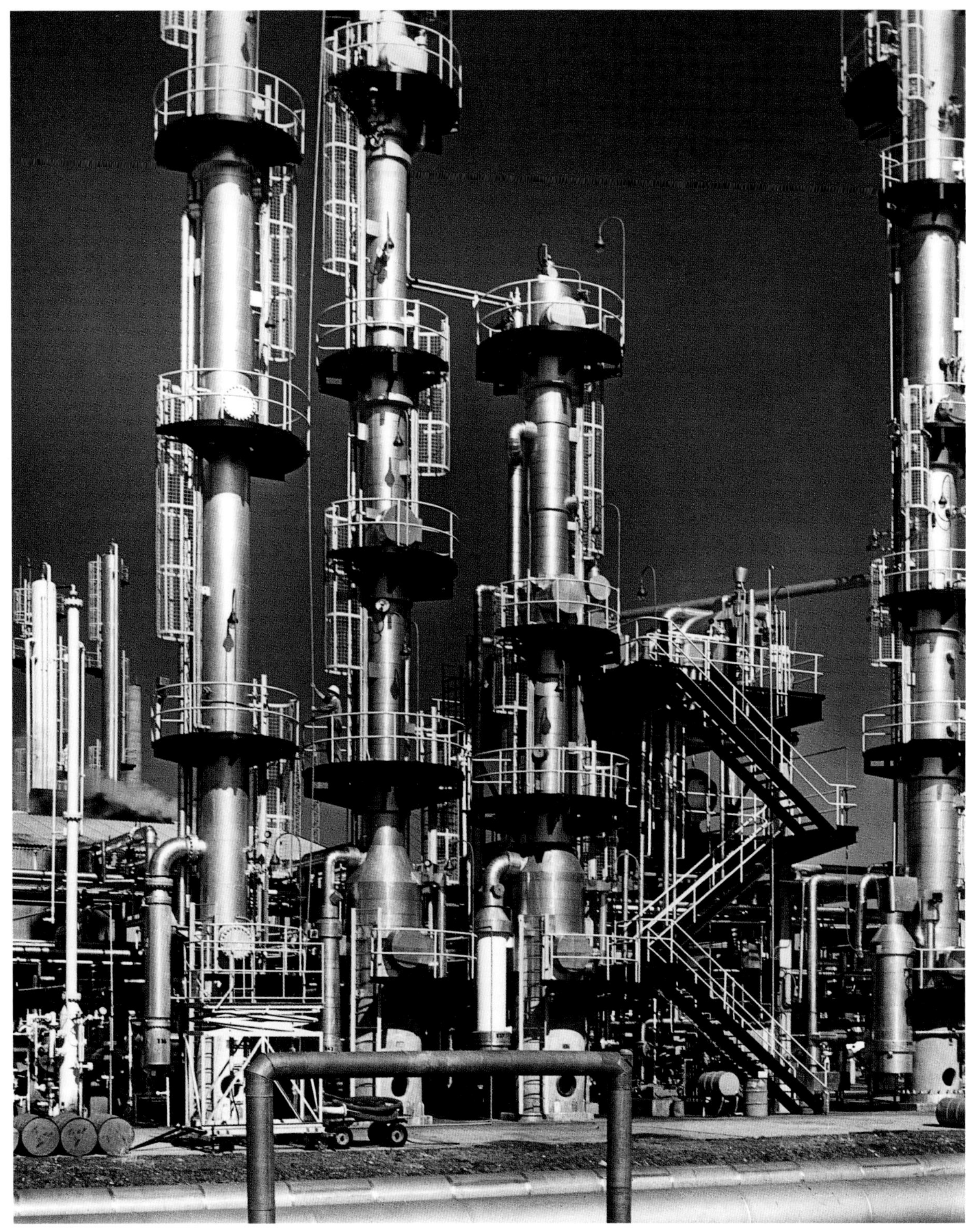

Shell Chemical Plant, Sydney, New South Wales 1961
gelatin silver photograph; 25 × 19.5cm
nla.cat-vn3415537

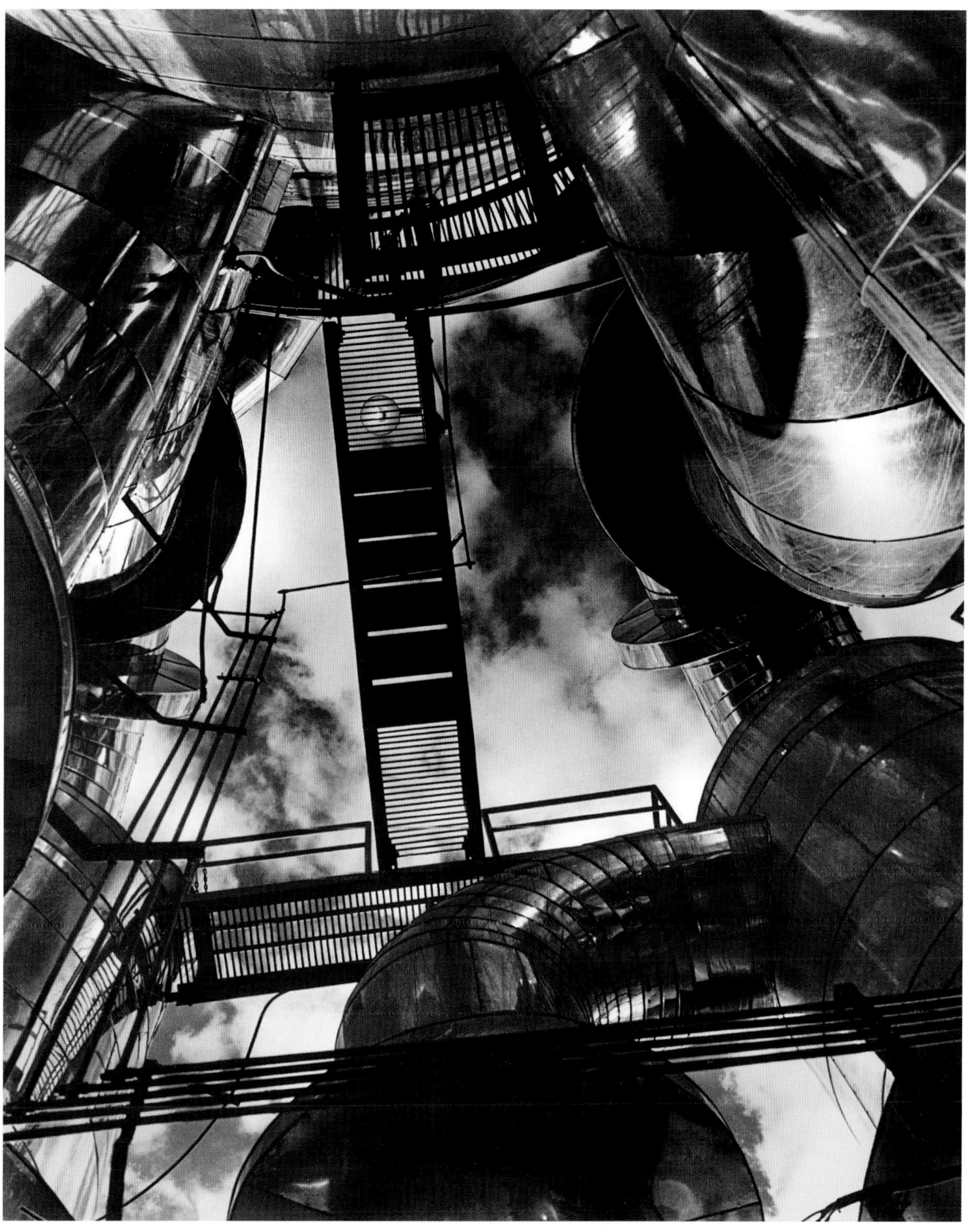

Sulphuric Acid Plant, Electrolytic Industries, Risdon, Tasmania 1959
gelatin silver photograph; 49.9 × 39.5cm
nla.cat-vn712328

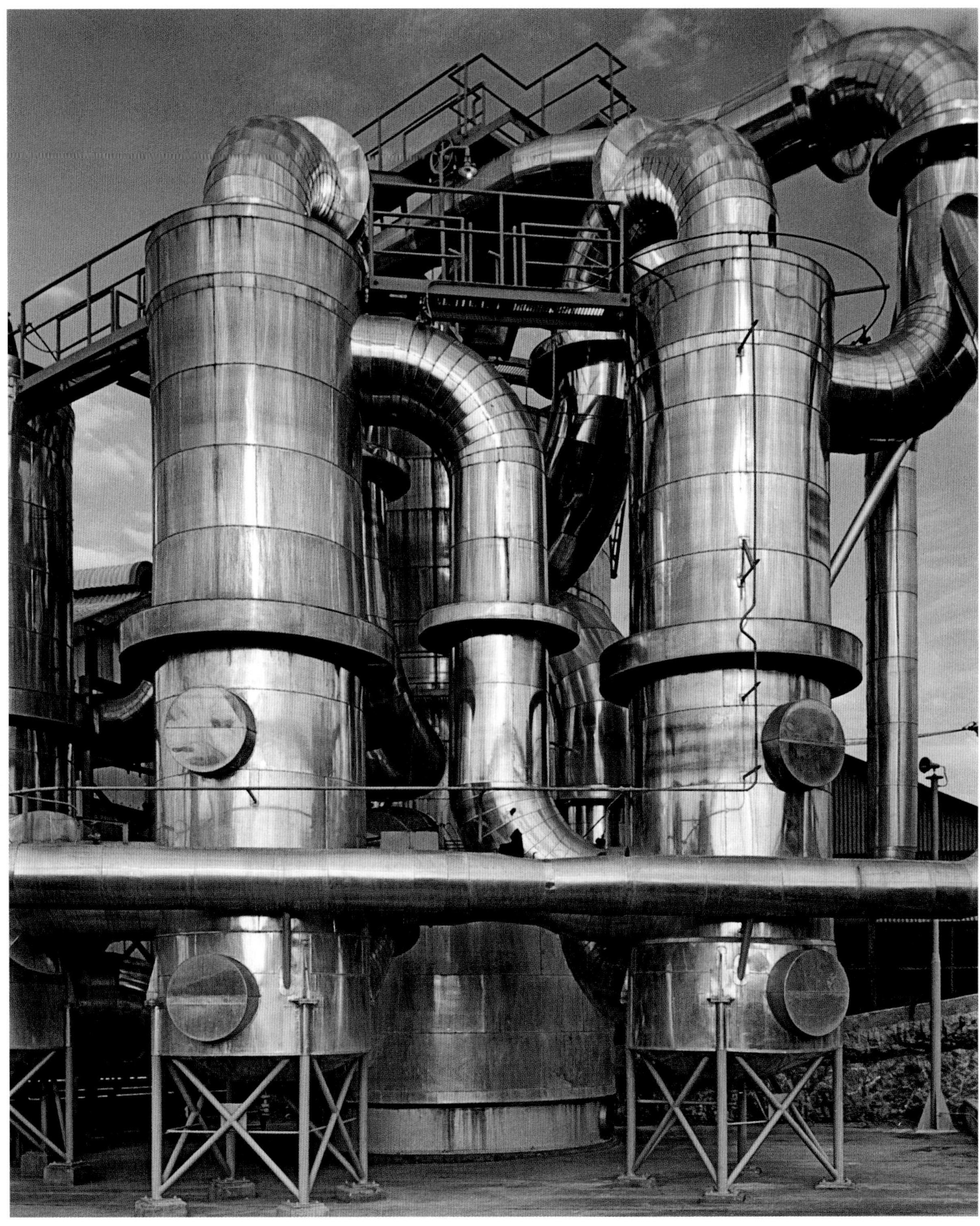

Electrolytic Zinc Sulphuric Acid Plant, Risdon, Tasmania 1959
gelatin silver photograph; 24.2 × 19.5cm
nla.cat-vn4281674

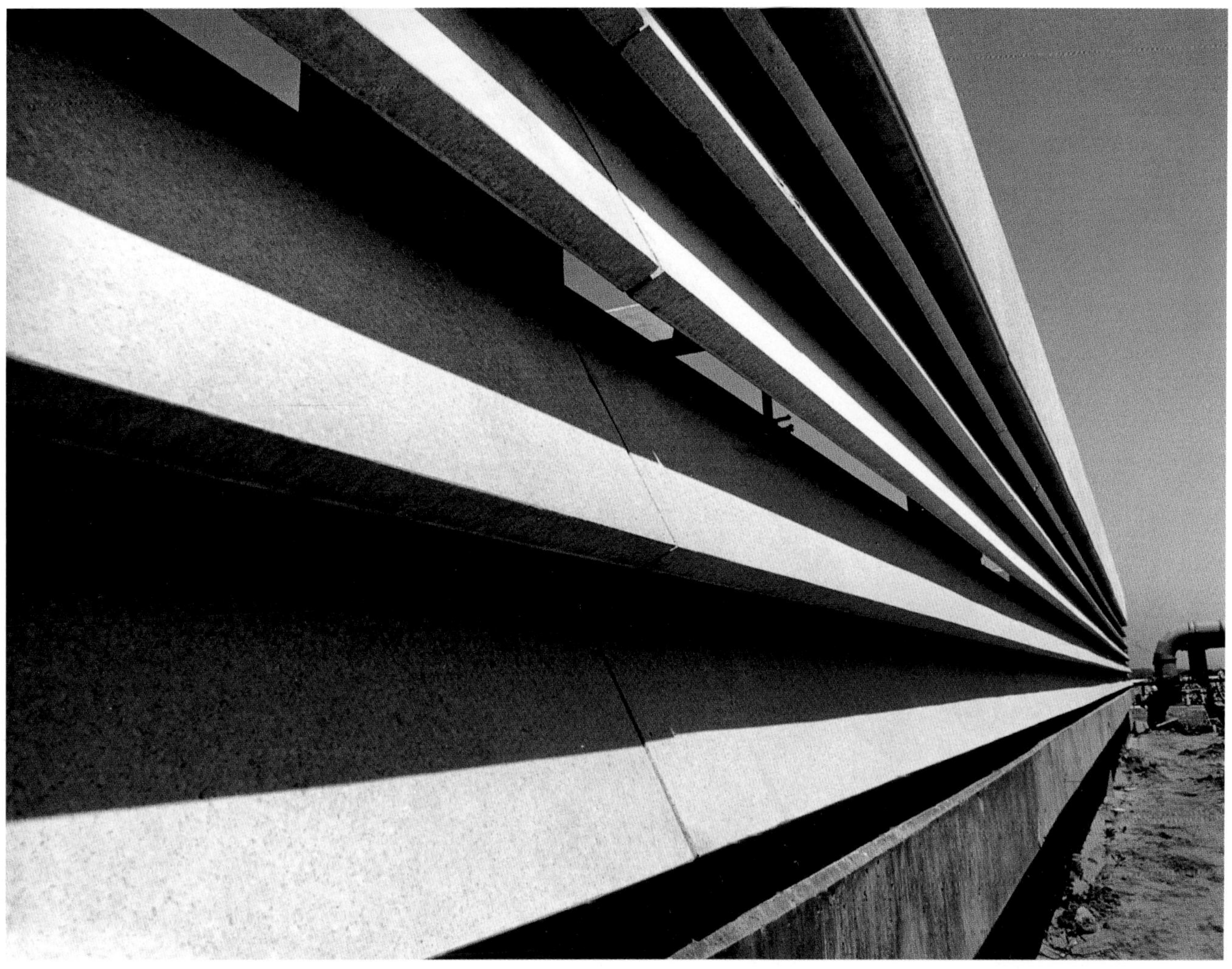

Construction of the South Eastern Purification Plant, Melbourne and Metropolitan Board of Works, Carrum, Victoria 1974 [38]
gelatin silver photograph; 19.2 × 24.5cm
nla.cat-vn3417710

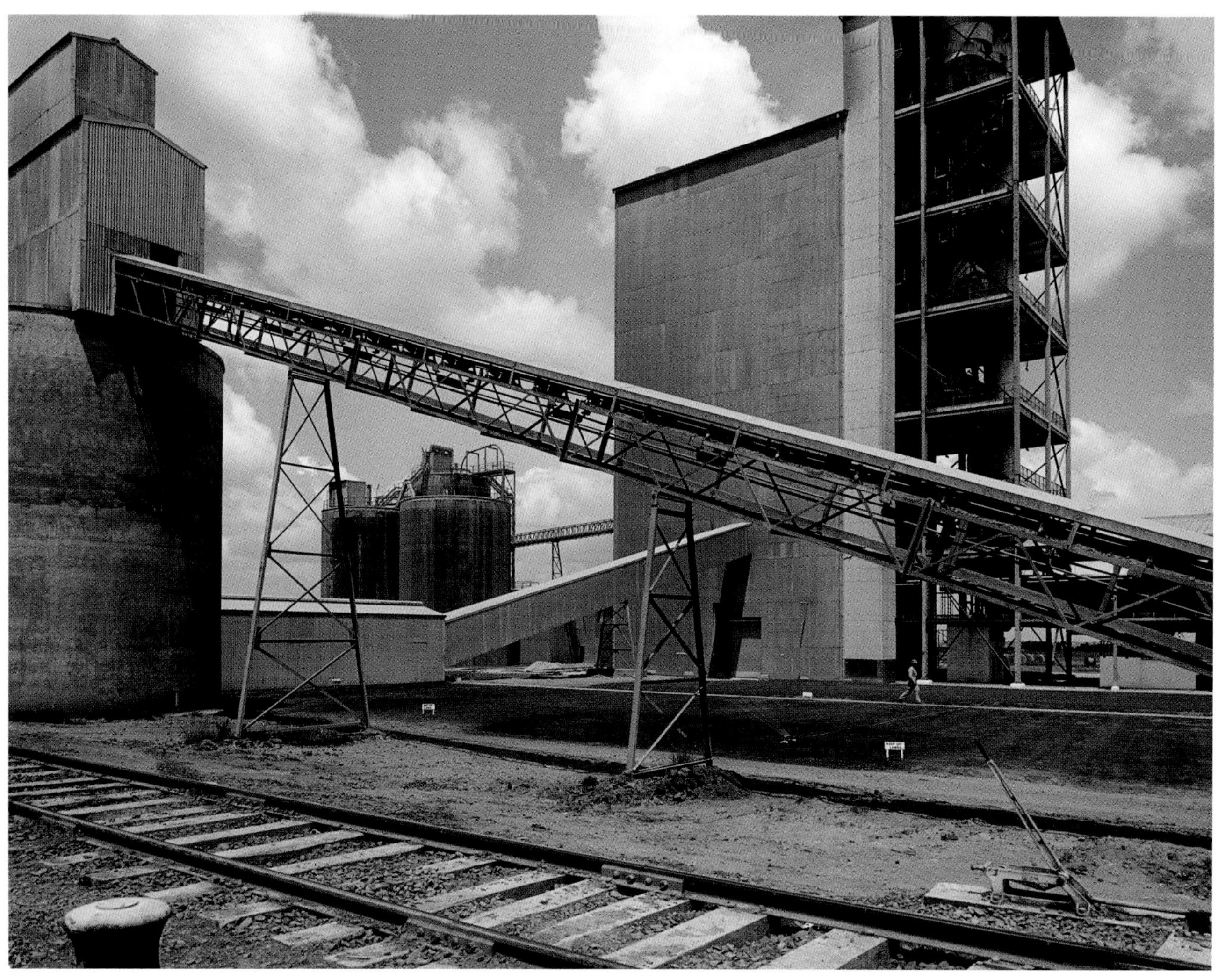

[Exterior of the Cement Plant] Victorian Portland Cement, Geelong, Victoria 1964
gelatin silver photograph; 19 × 24cm
nla.cat-vn3457430

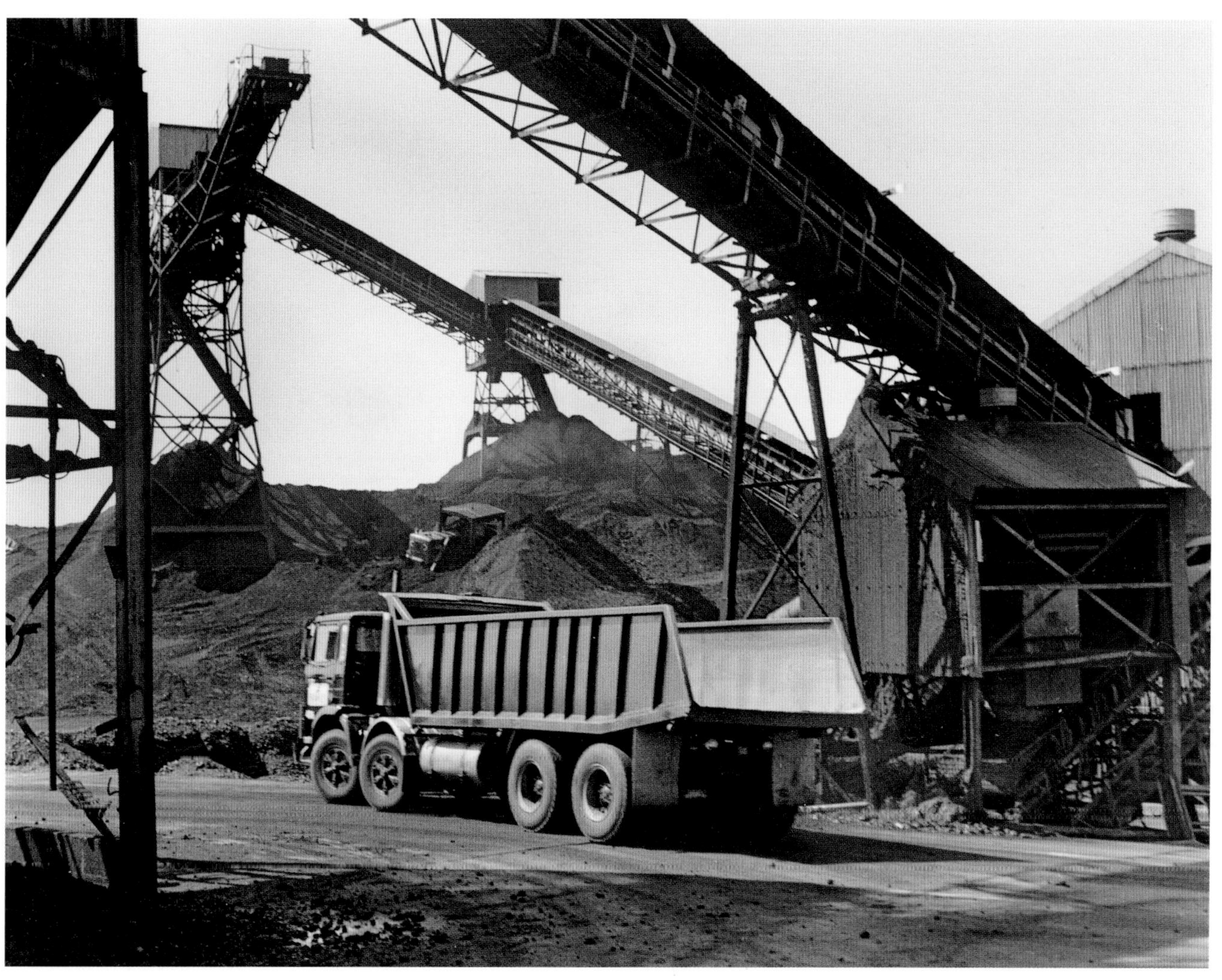

Coal Trucks About to Be Loaded, Belambi Coal Mine, New South Wales 1985
gelatin silver photograph; 19.5 × 24.5cm
nla.cat-vn1117269

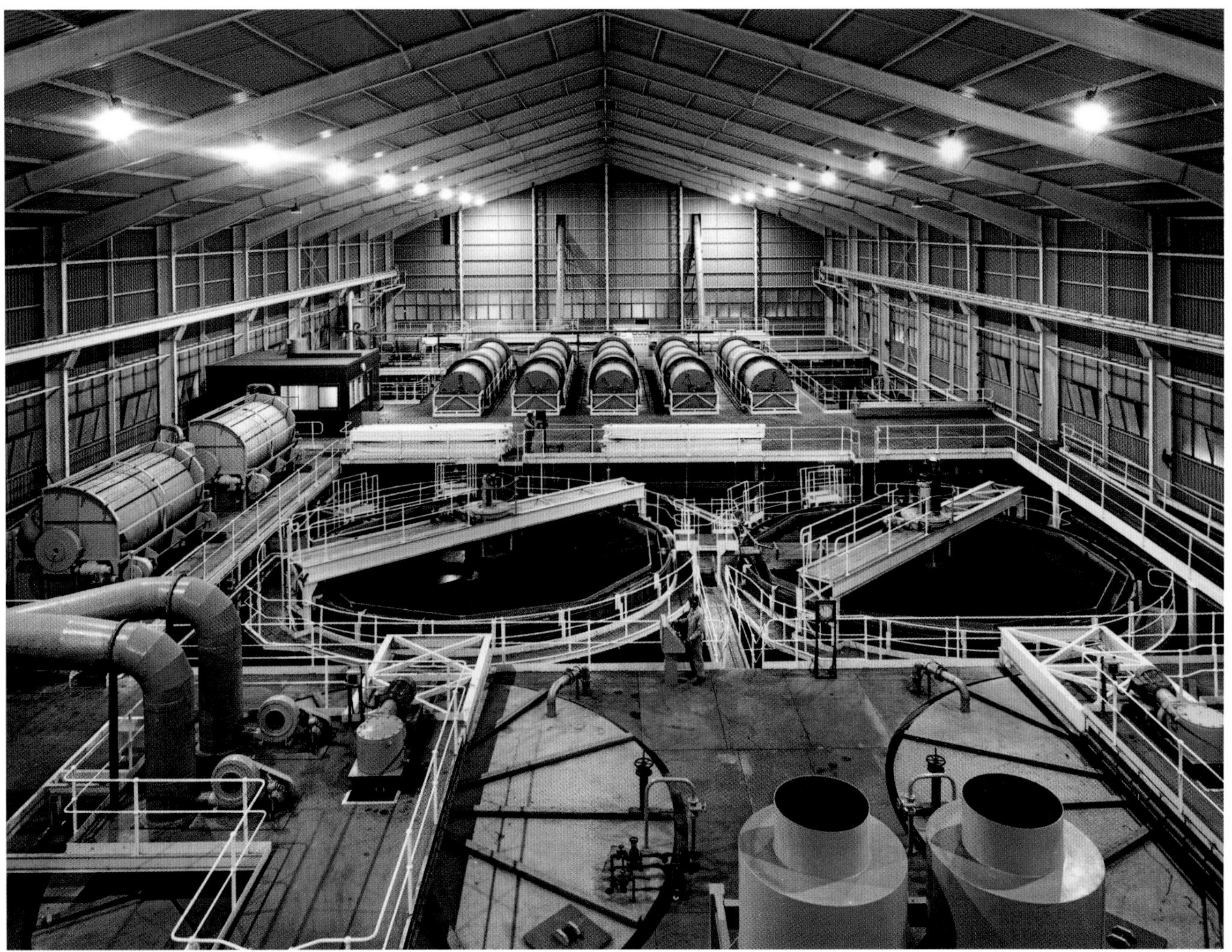

BHAS, Pt Pirie, South Australia 1967
gelatin silver photograph; 19.3 × 24.7cm
nla.cat-vn2828931

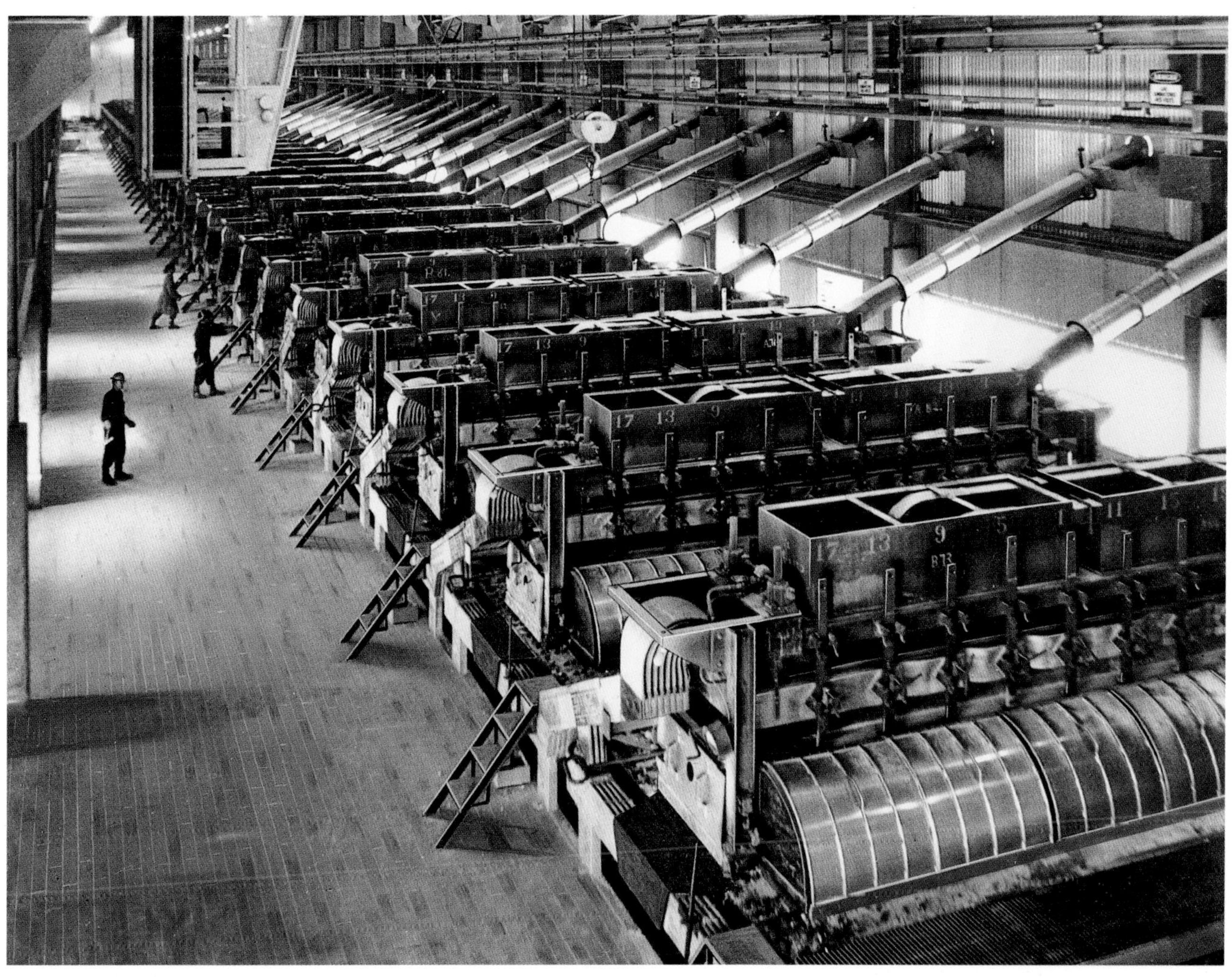

Potline at Comalco's Aluminium Smelters, Bell Bay, Tasmania 1962
gelatin silver photograph; 19.6 × 24.9cm
nla.cat-vn4281418

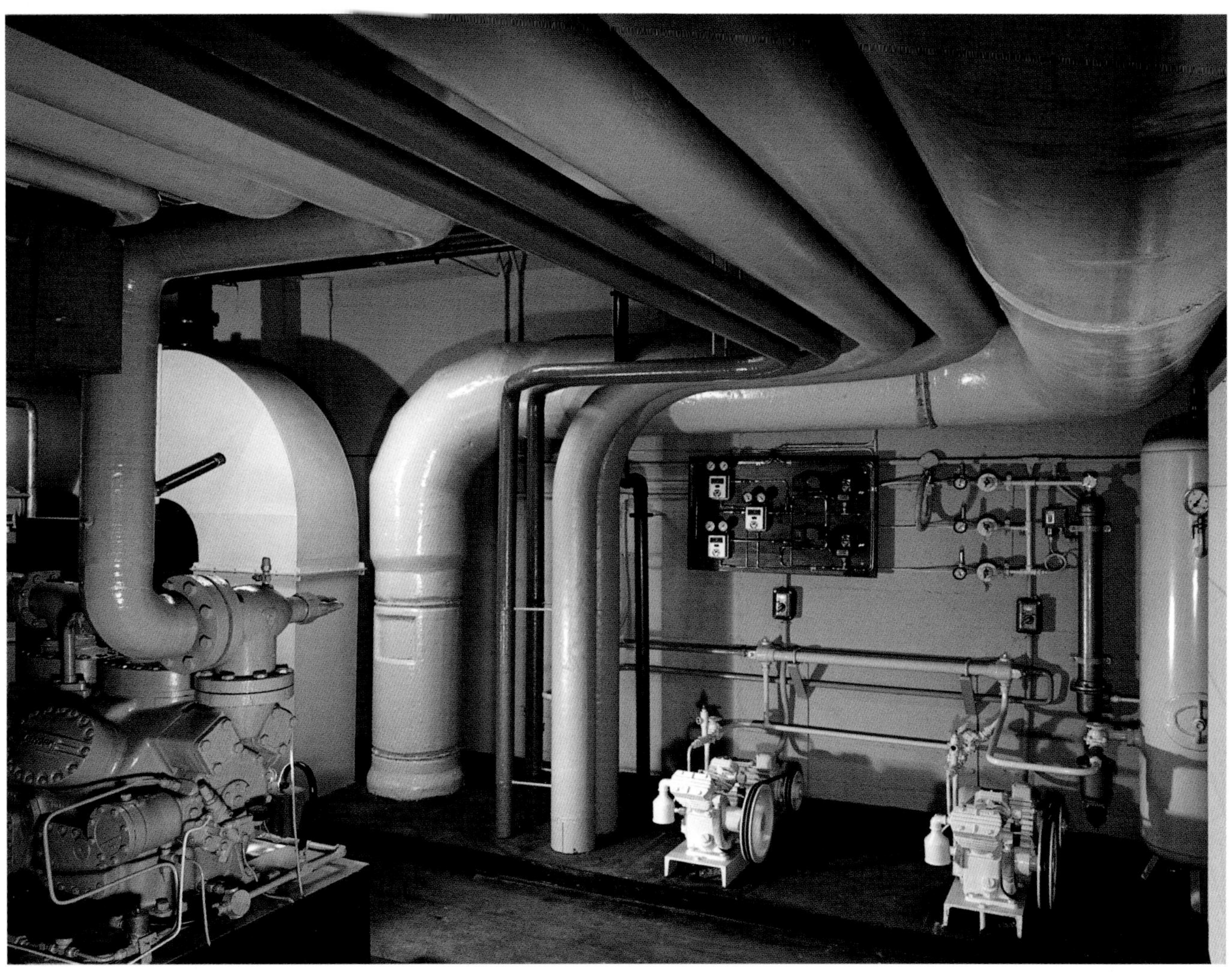

Boiler Room at the South British Insurance Company, Melbourne, Victoria, Architects Bates, Smart and McCutcheon 1961
gelatin silver photograph; 19.5 × 24cm
nla.cat-vn3060520

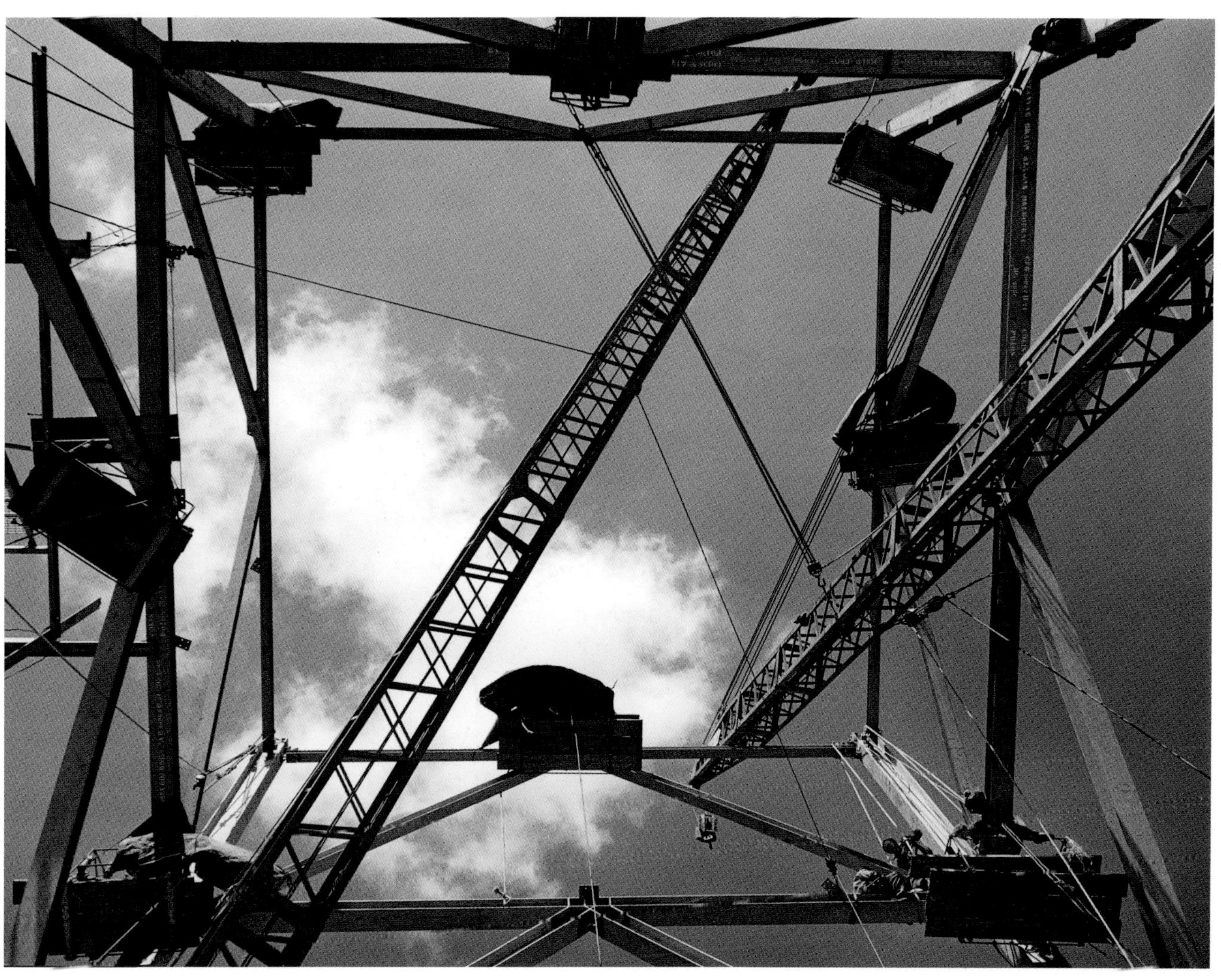

[Skyward View of Cranes at] Stanvac Oil Refinery, Altona, Victoria 1954
gelatin silver photograph; 19.6 × 24.5cm
nla.cat-vn3419730

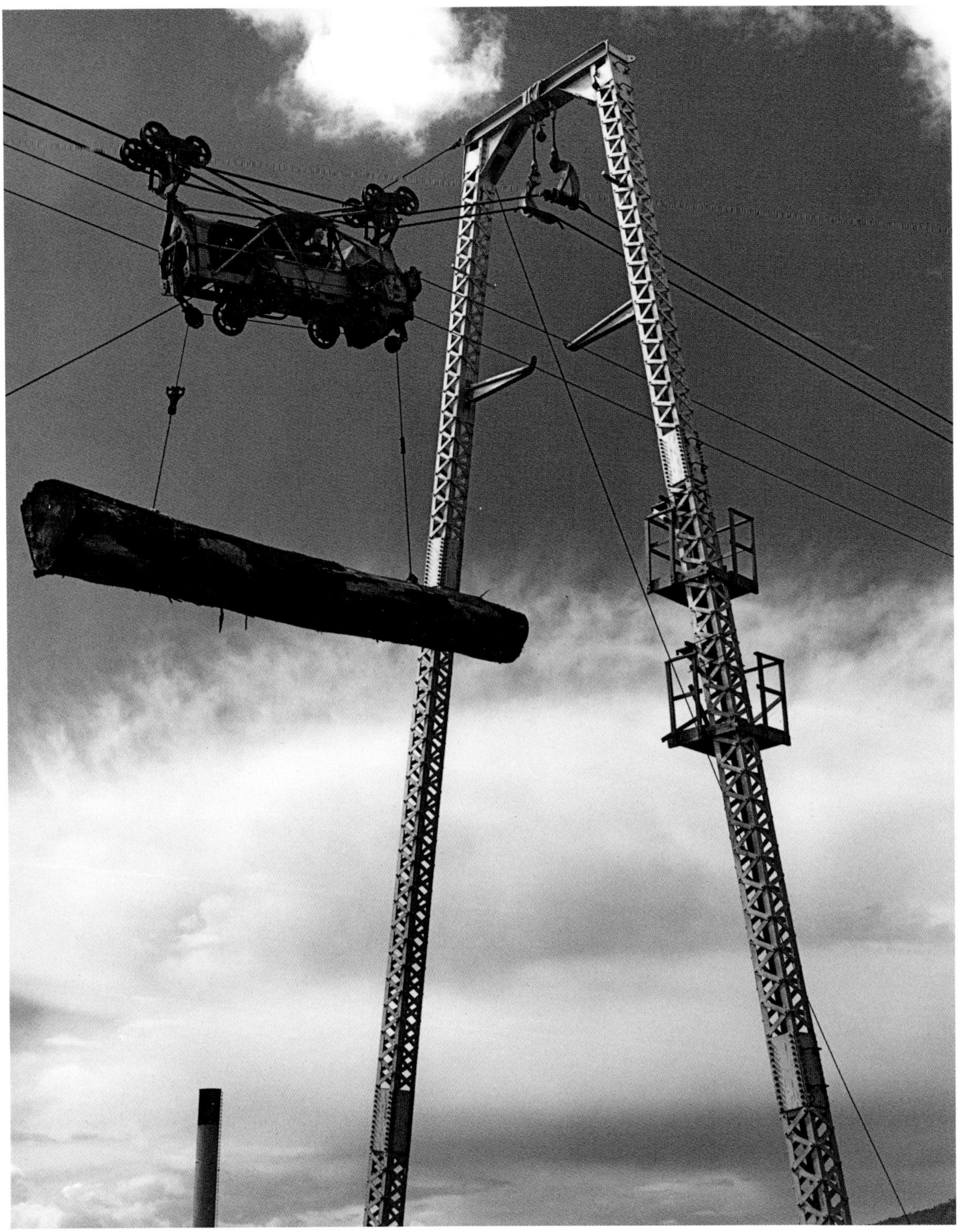

Associated Pulp and Paper Mills Timber Industry Near Burnie, Tasmania 1956
gelatin silver photograph; 24.6 × 19cm
nla.cat-vn13211

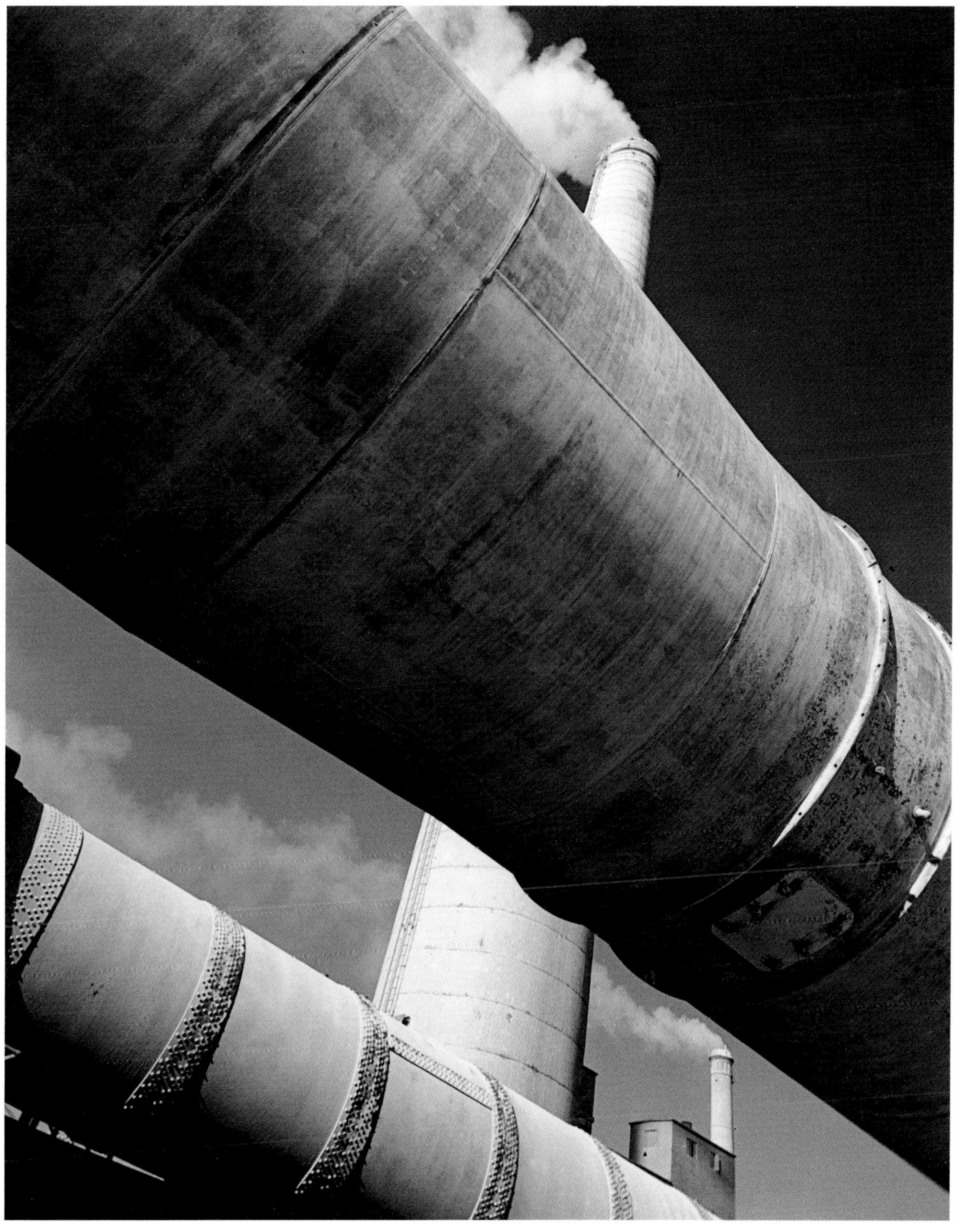

Australian Cement, Geelong, Victoria 1962
gelatin silver photograph; 24.2 × 18.8cm
nla.cat-vn3943074

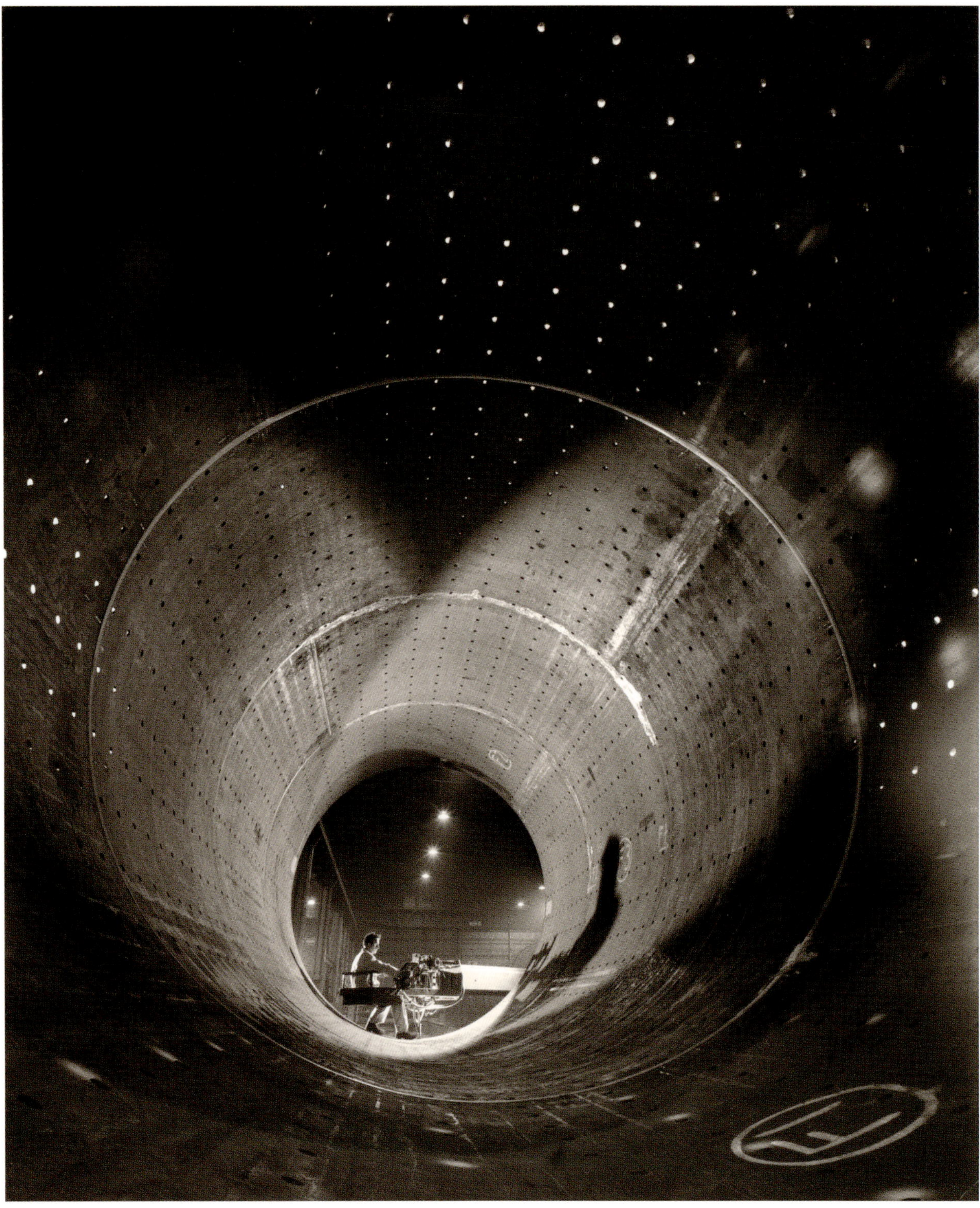

Cement Mill, Vickers Ruwolt, Burnley, Victoria 1969
gelatin silver photograph; 49.6 × 39.3cm
nla.cat-vn343415

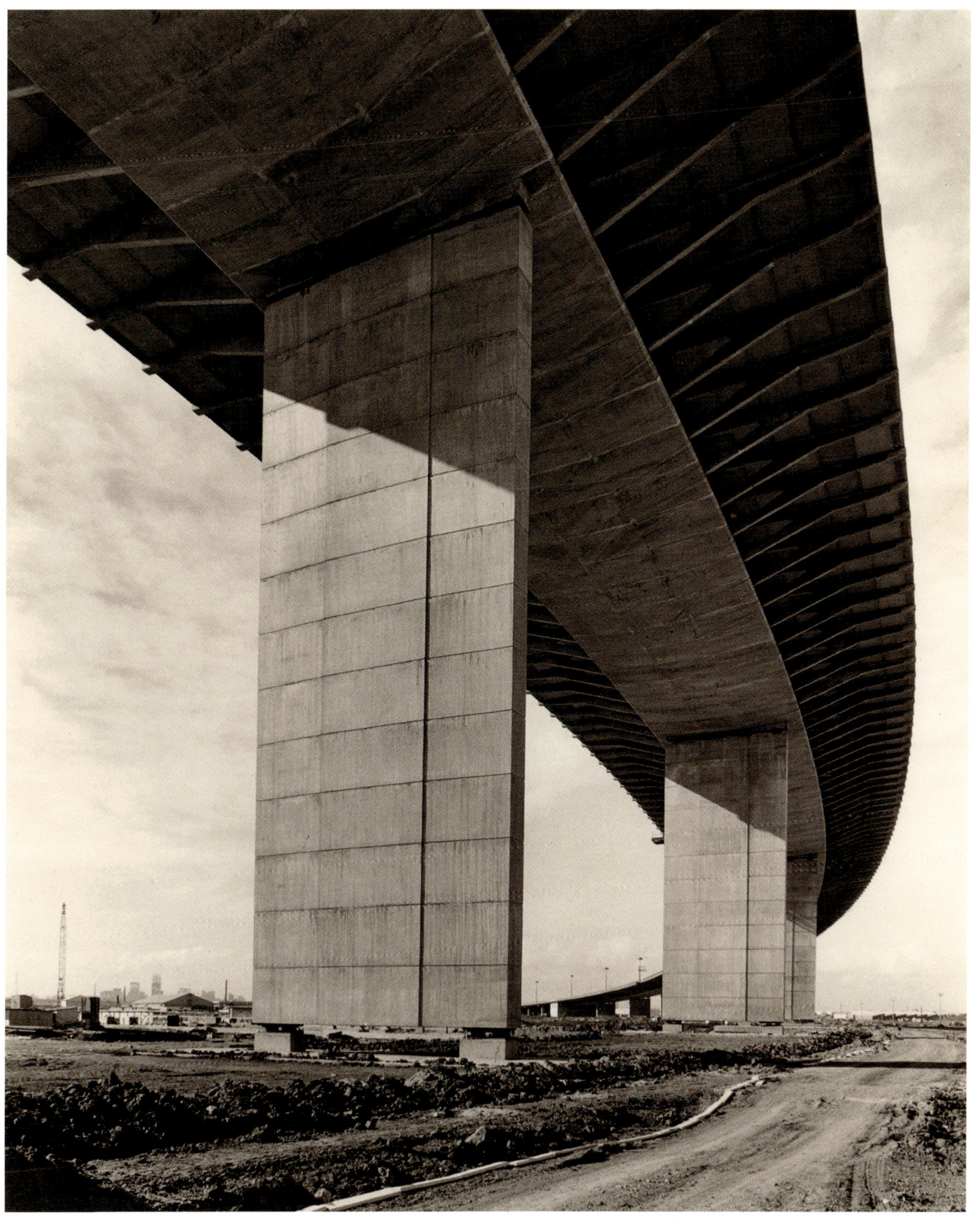

Westgate Bridge, Melbourne, Victoria 1971
gelatin silver photograph; 50.3 × 40cm
nla.cat-vn1096461

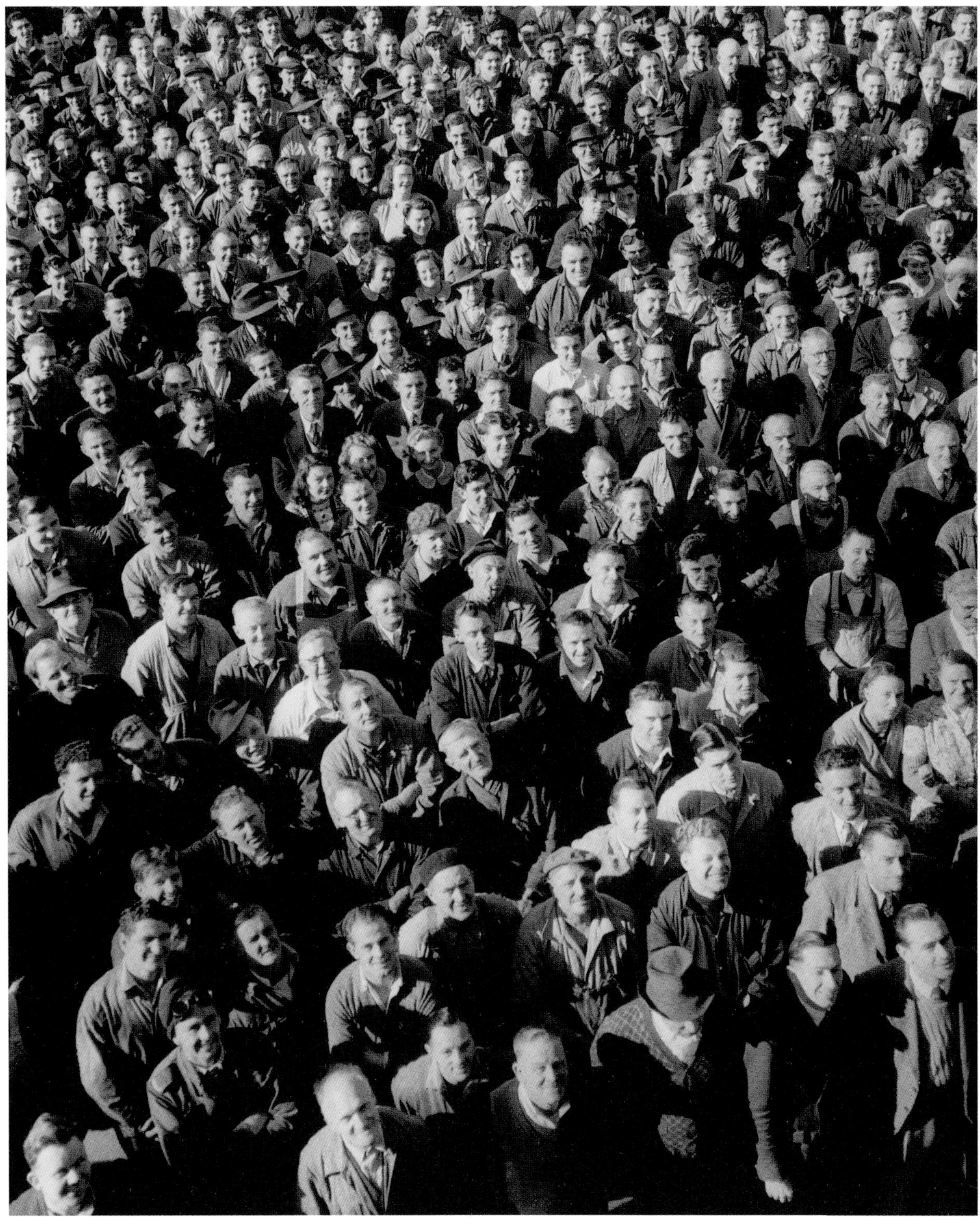

Shift Change at Kelly and Lewis Engineering Works, Springvale, Victoria 1949
gelatin silver photograph; 25.6 × 19cm
nla.cat-vn4549631

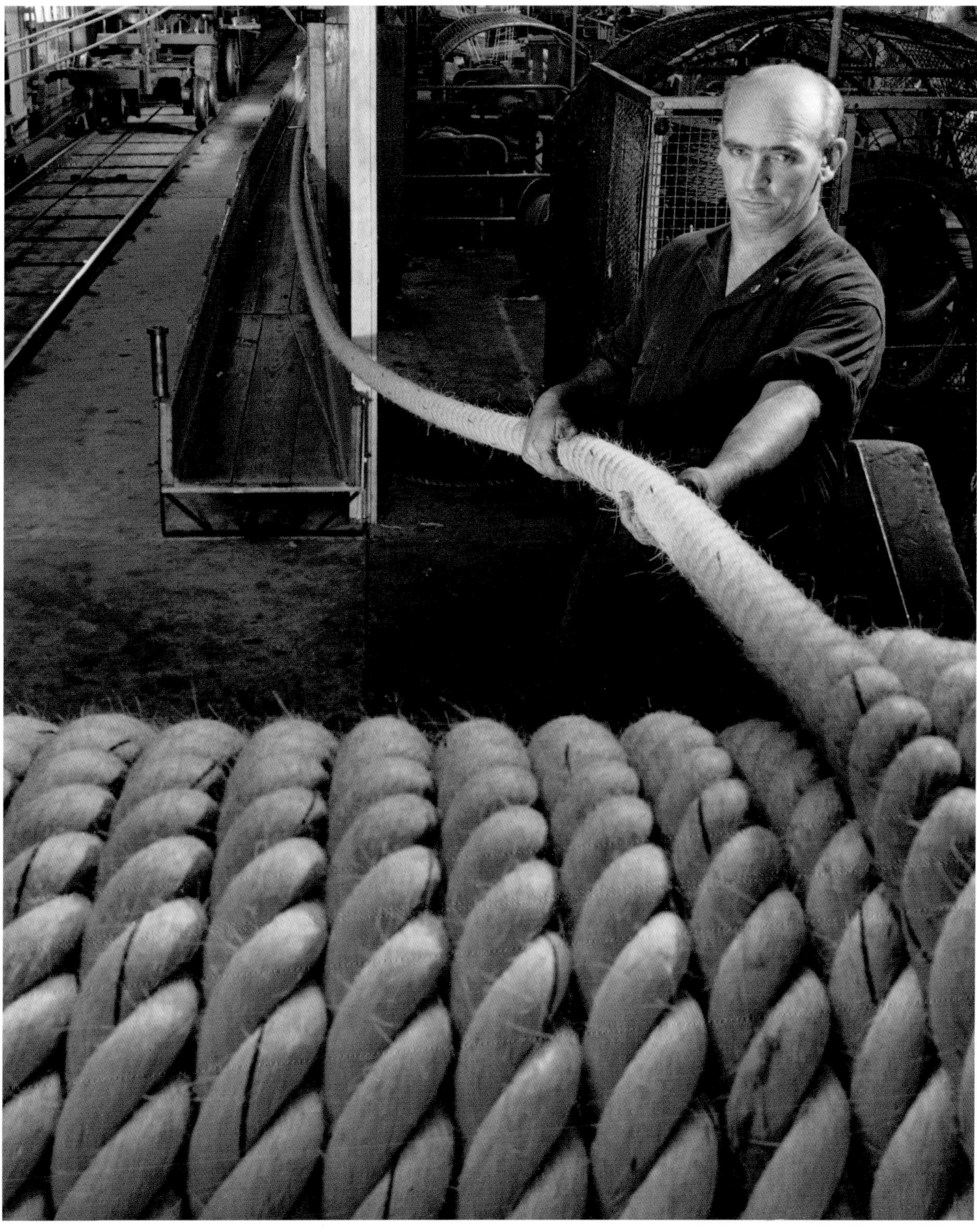

Employee Making Rope with Ropeway at Miller Rope, Brunswick, Victoria 1962
gelatin silver photograph; 24.5 × 19.5cm
nla.cat-vn4495586

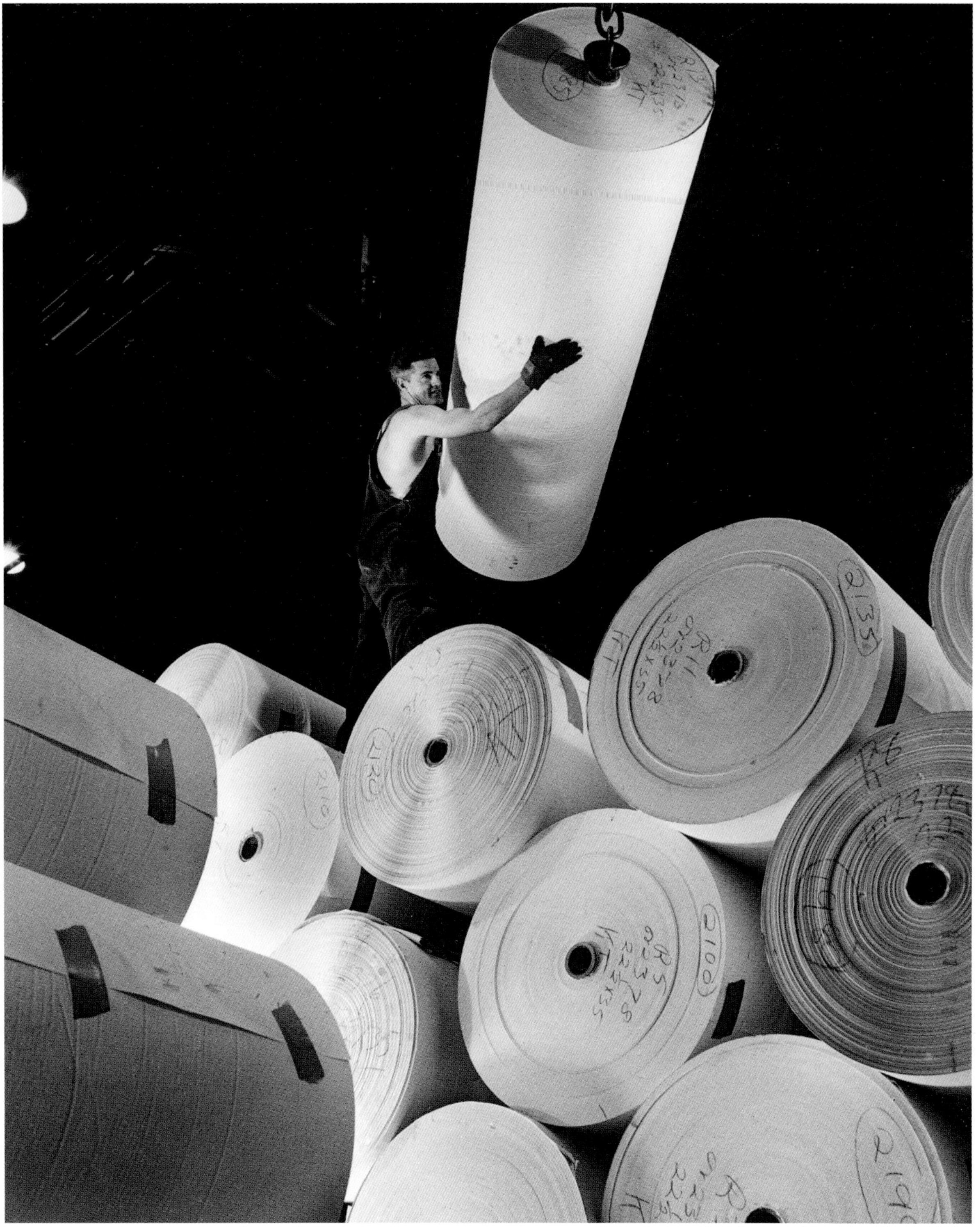

Associated Pulp and Paper Mills, Burnie, Tasmania 1956
gelatin silver photograph; 50 × 40.4cm
nla.cat-vn2234124

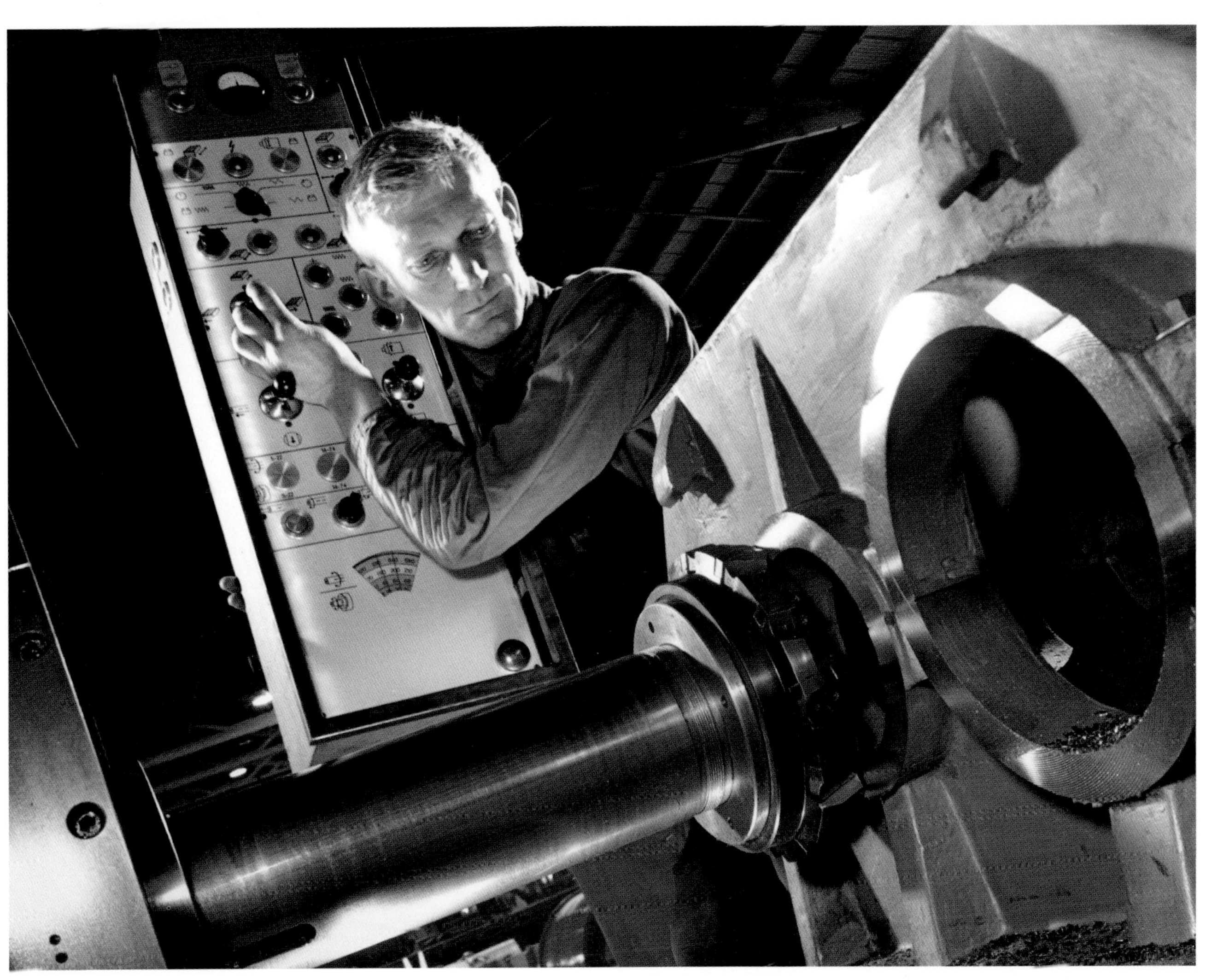

Worker Operating Metal Lathe, Marweight Engineering, Melbourne, Victoria 1968
gelatin silver photograph; 19.7 × 24.6cm
nla.cat-vn4551493

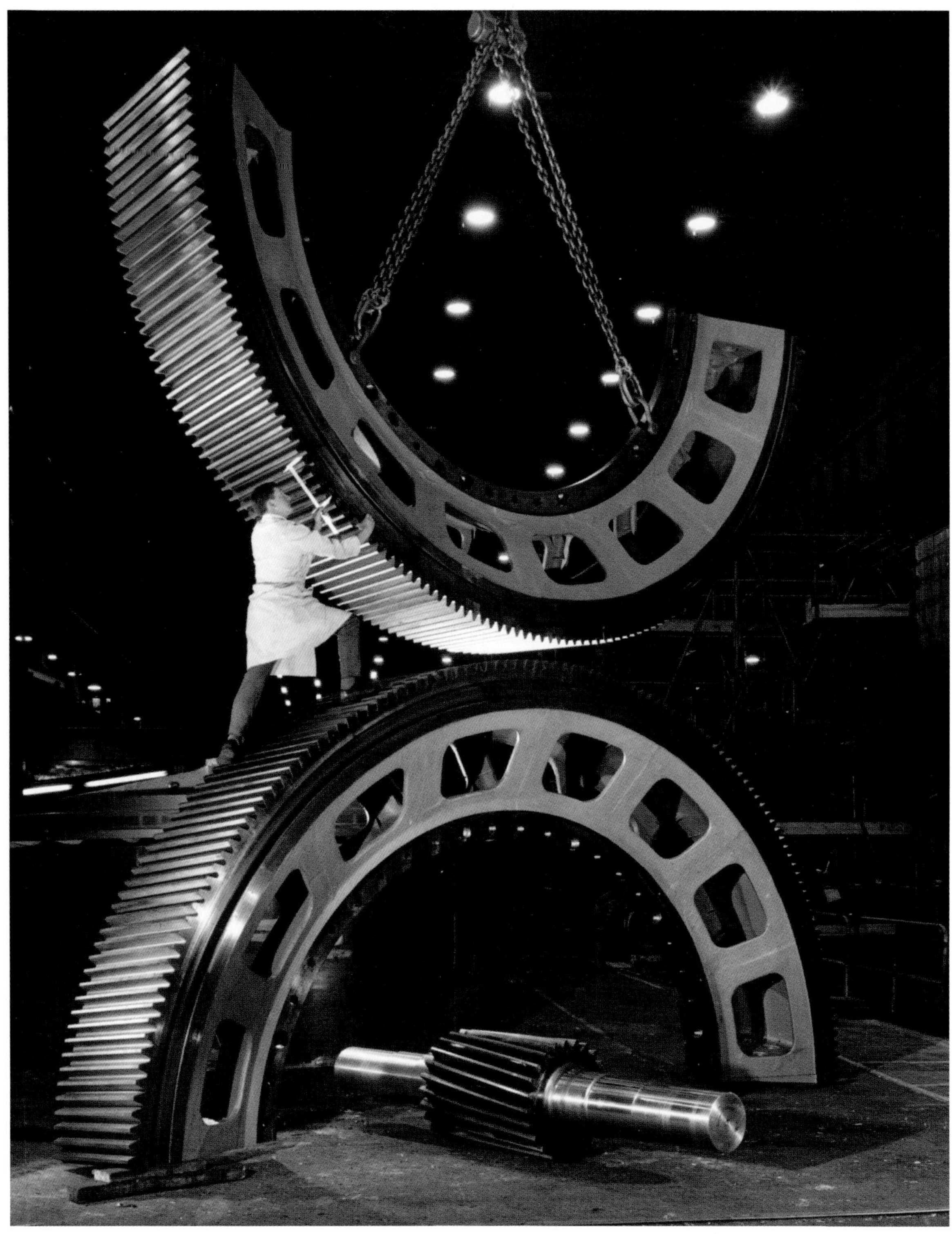

Gears for the Mining Industry, Vickers Ruwolt, Burnley, Victoria 1967
gelatin silver photograph; 49.6 × 39.3cm
nla.cat-vn1859962

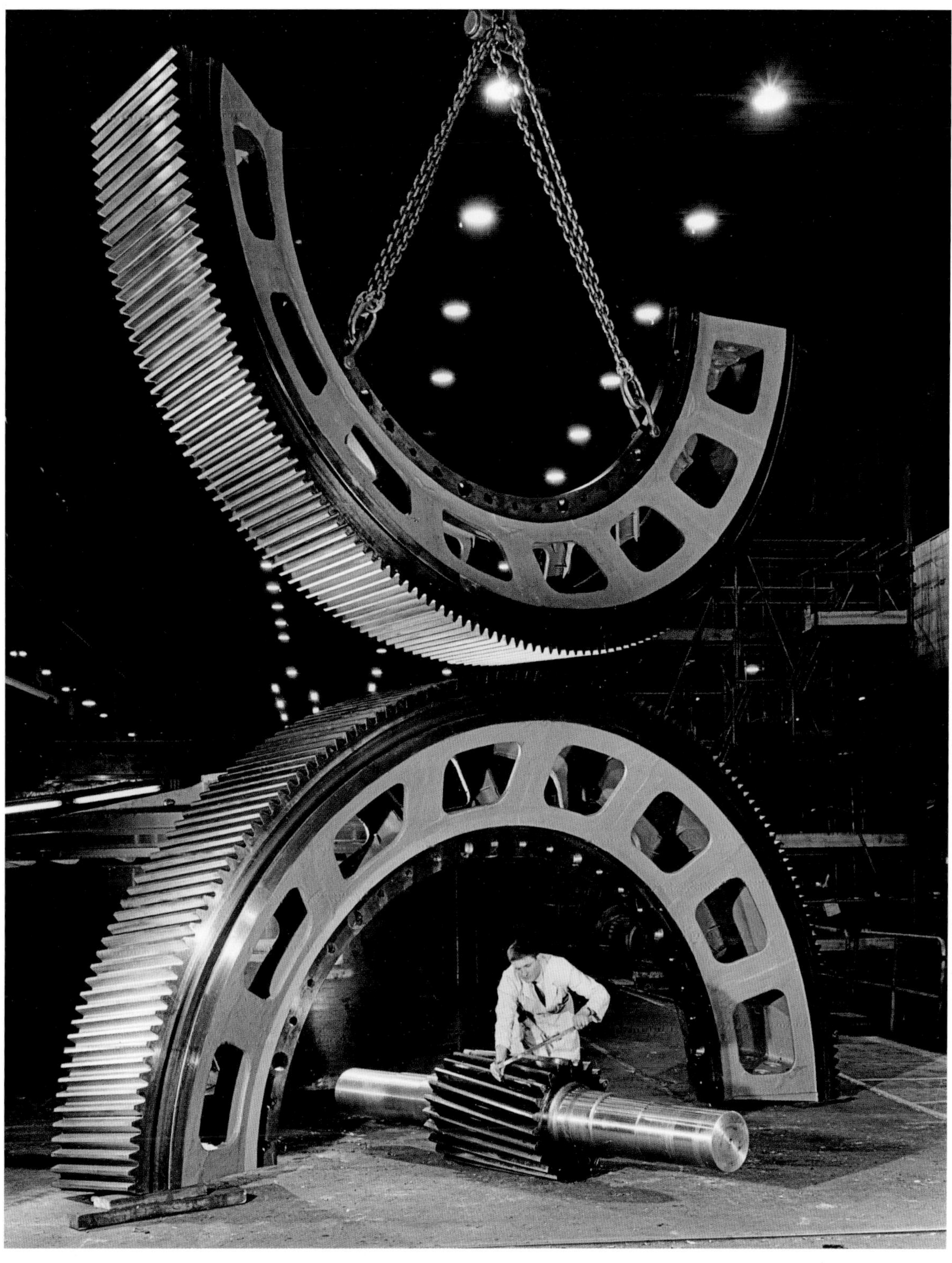

Gears for the Mining Industry, Vickers Ruwolt, Burnley, Victoria 1967
gelatin silver photograph; 24.6 × 19cm
nla.cat-vn3427959

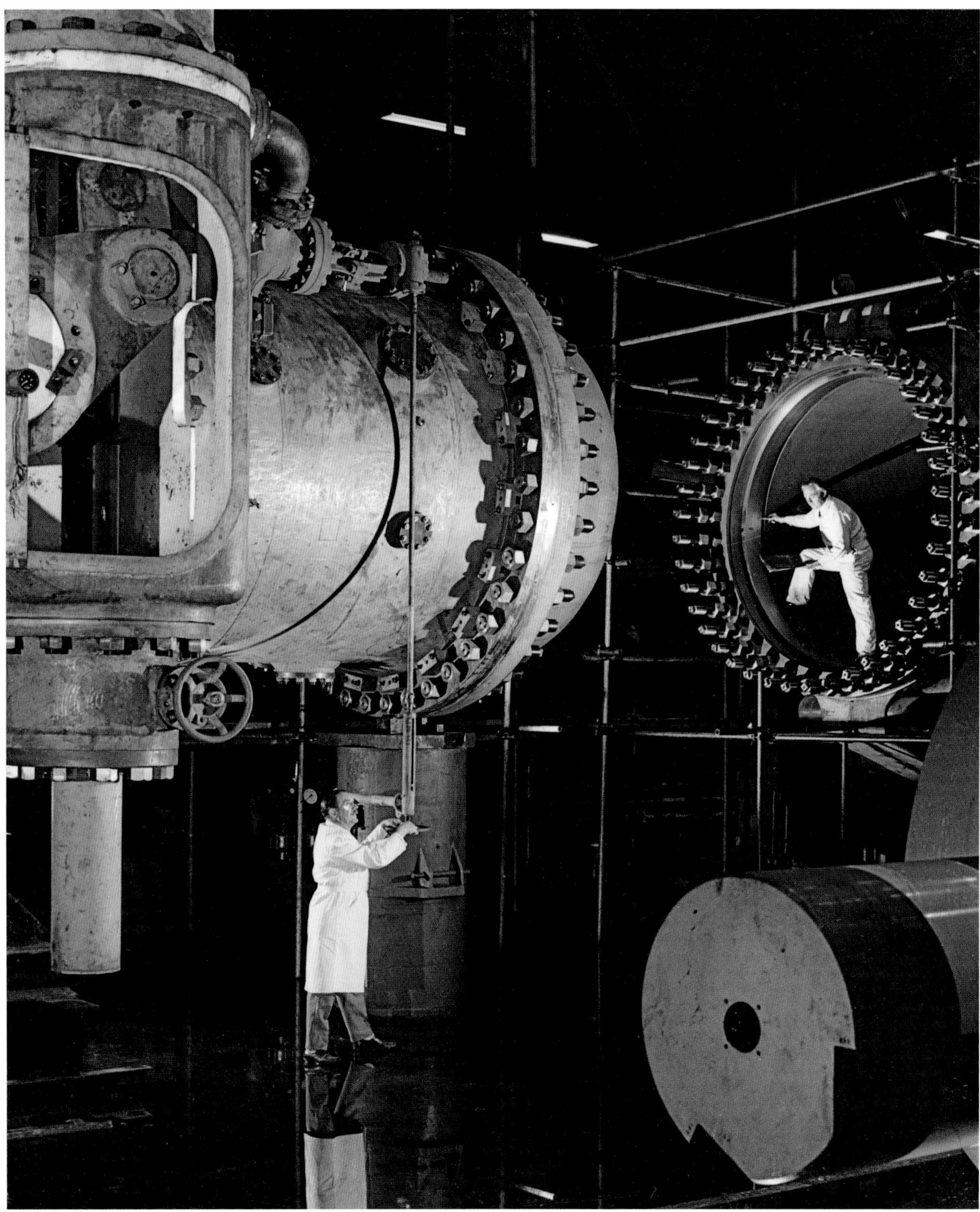

Hitashi Valves from Snowy Mountains Hydroelectric Scheme, Vickers Ruwolt, Burnley, Victoria 1967
gelatin silver photograph; 24.5 × 19.8cm
nla.cat-vn3427968

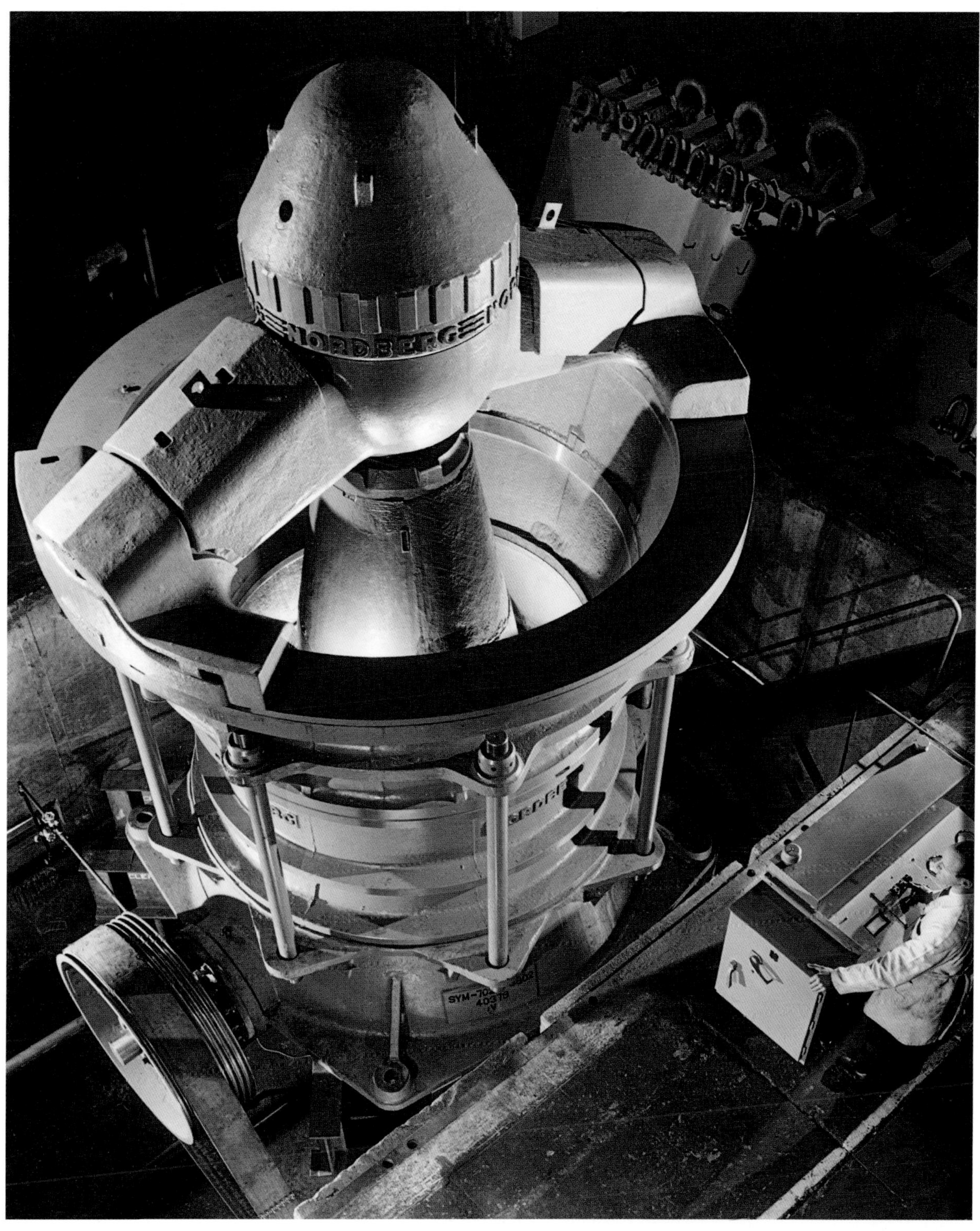

Nordberg Ore Crusher for the Mining Industry, Vickers Ruwolt, Burnley, Victoria 1969
gelatin silver photograph; 49.8 × 38.8cm
nla.cat-vn714991

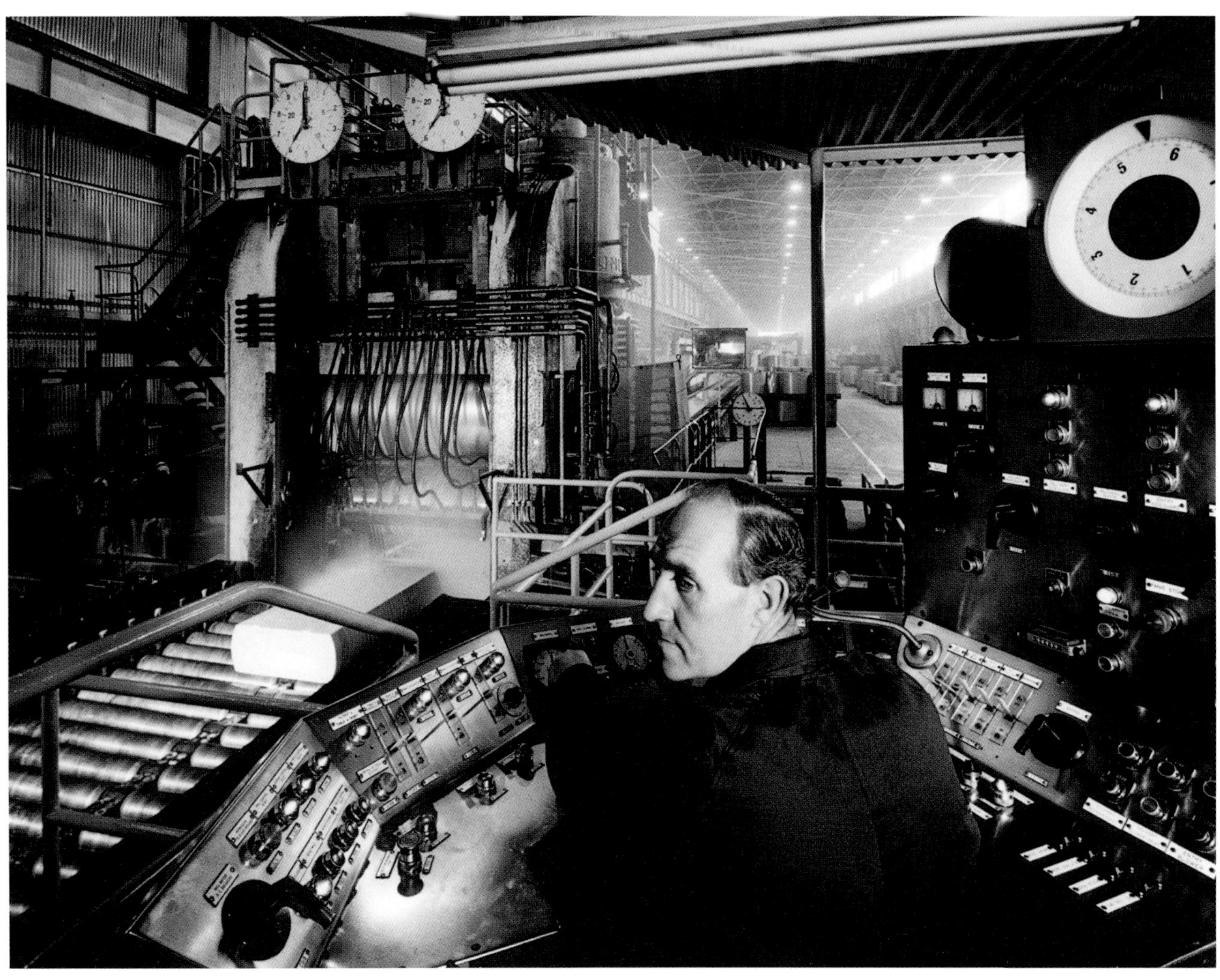

Control Cabin Operator, Hot Reversing Mill, Alcoa, Point Henry, Geelong, Victoria 1970
gelatin silver photograph; 39.2 × 49.5cm
nla.cat-vn2237712

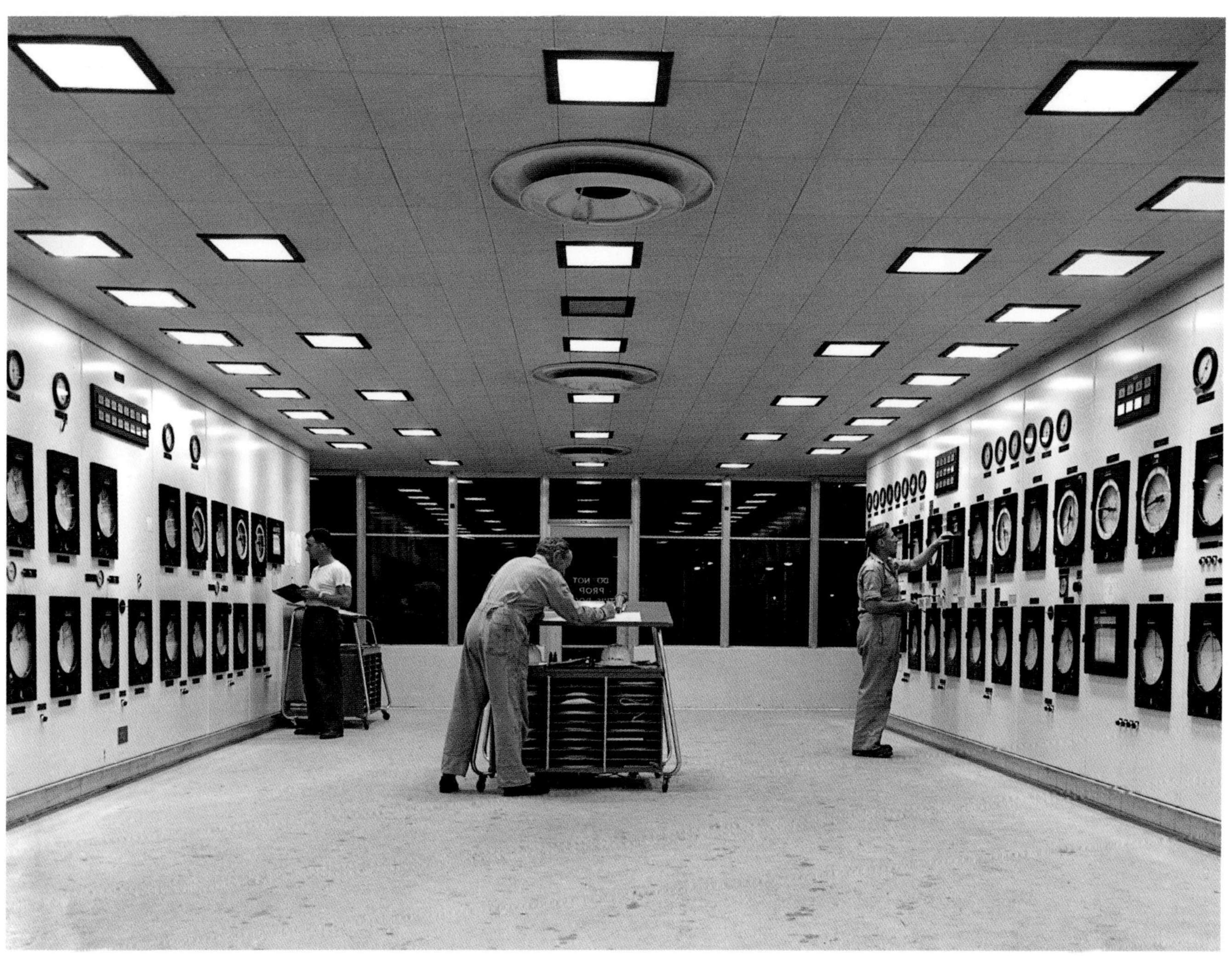

Central Control Room at Mobil's Stanvac Oil Refinery, Altona, Victoria 1956
gelatin silver photograph; 19.4 × 25cm
nla.cat-vn4804052

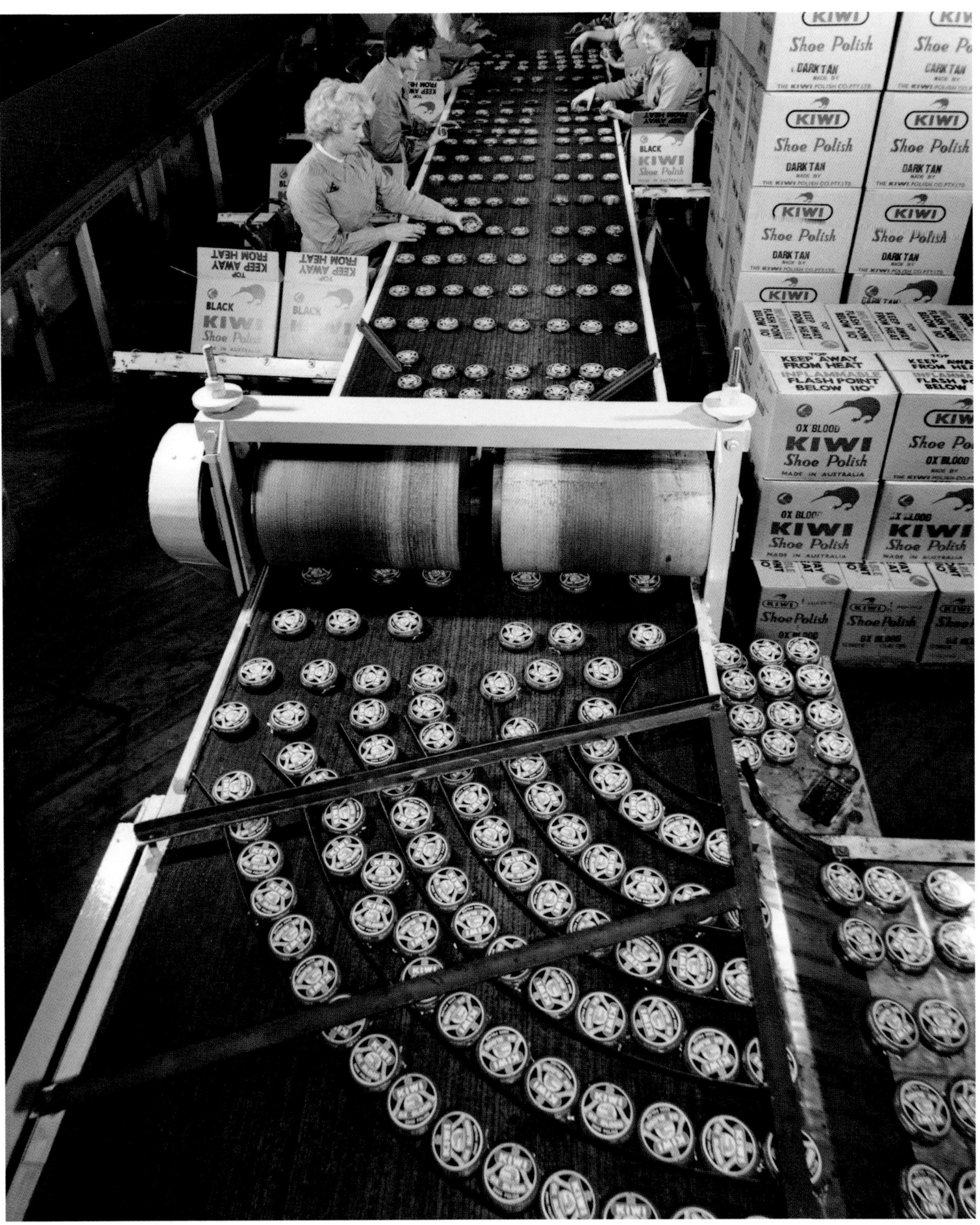

Packing Tins of Kiwi Shoe Polish at Burnley, Victoria 1962
gelatin silver photograph; 24 × 19cm
nla.cat-vn4551488

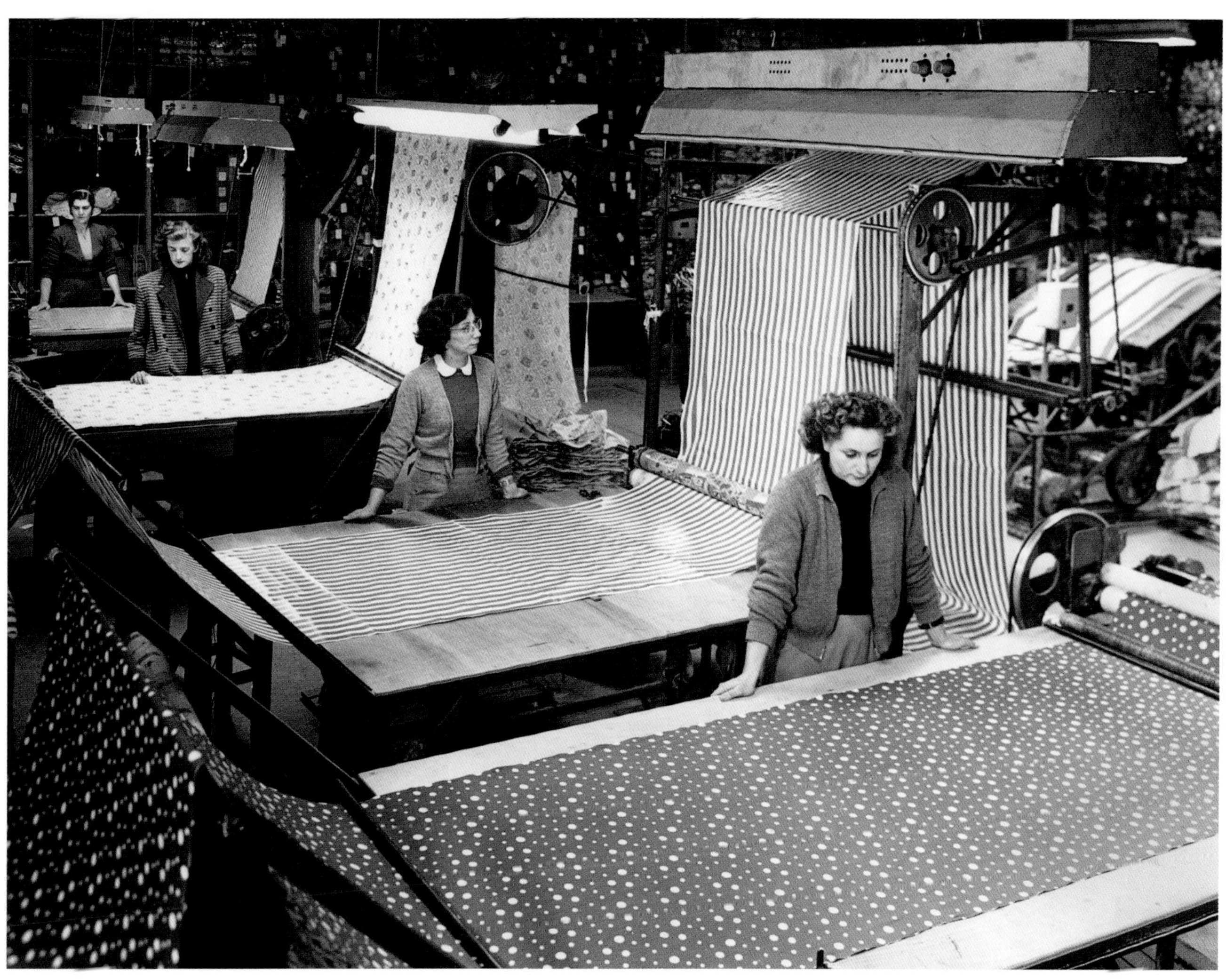

Colortex Fabrics, Melbourne, Victoria 1957
gelatin silver photograph; 38.7 × 49.5cm
nla.cat-vn3046177

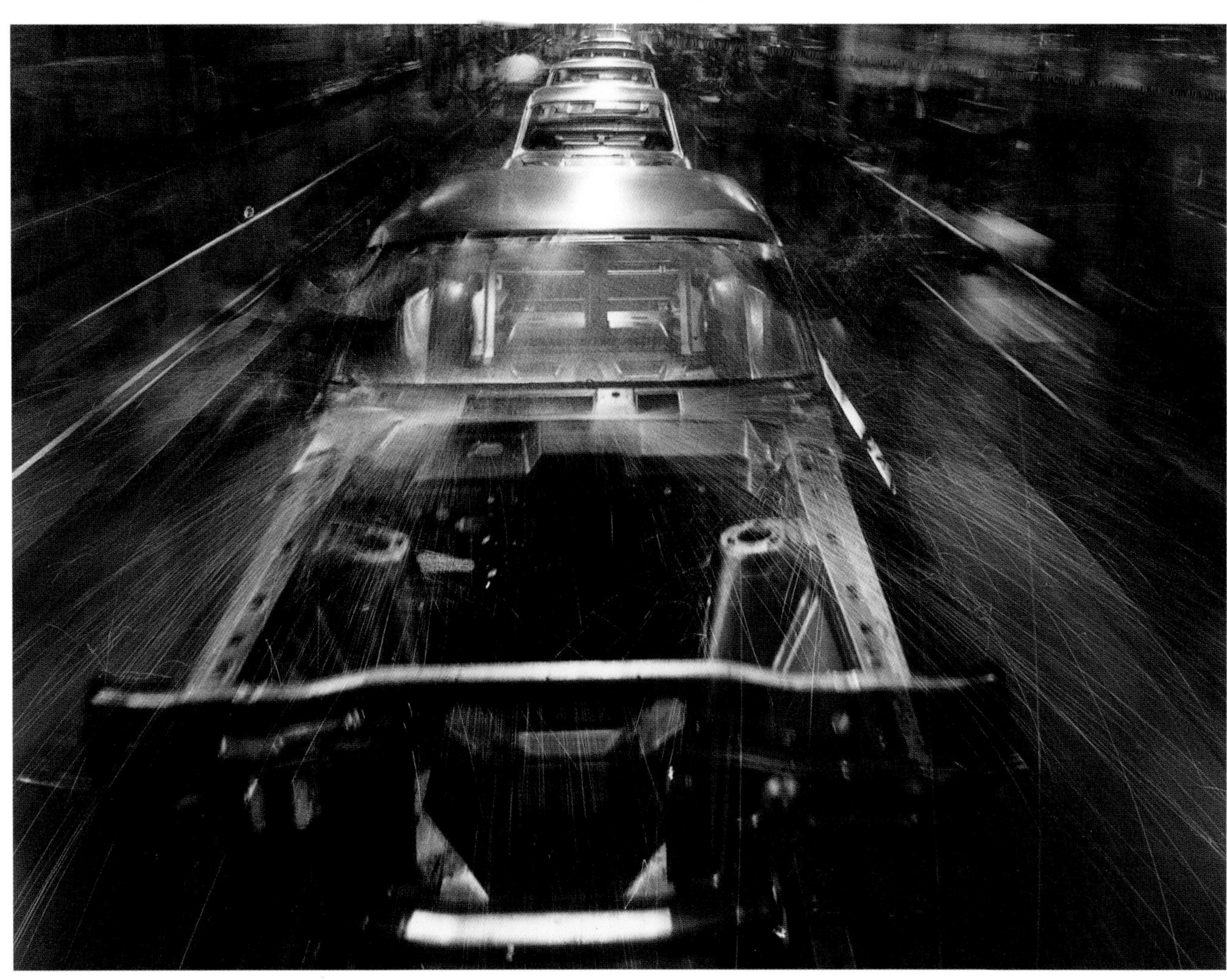

Assembly Line at Ford Motors, Broadmeadows, Victoria 1966
gelatin silver photograph; 39.2 × 49.8cm
nla.cat-vn714637

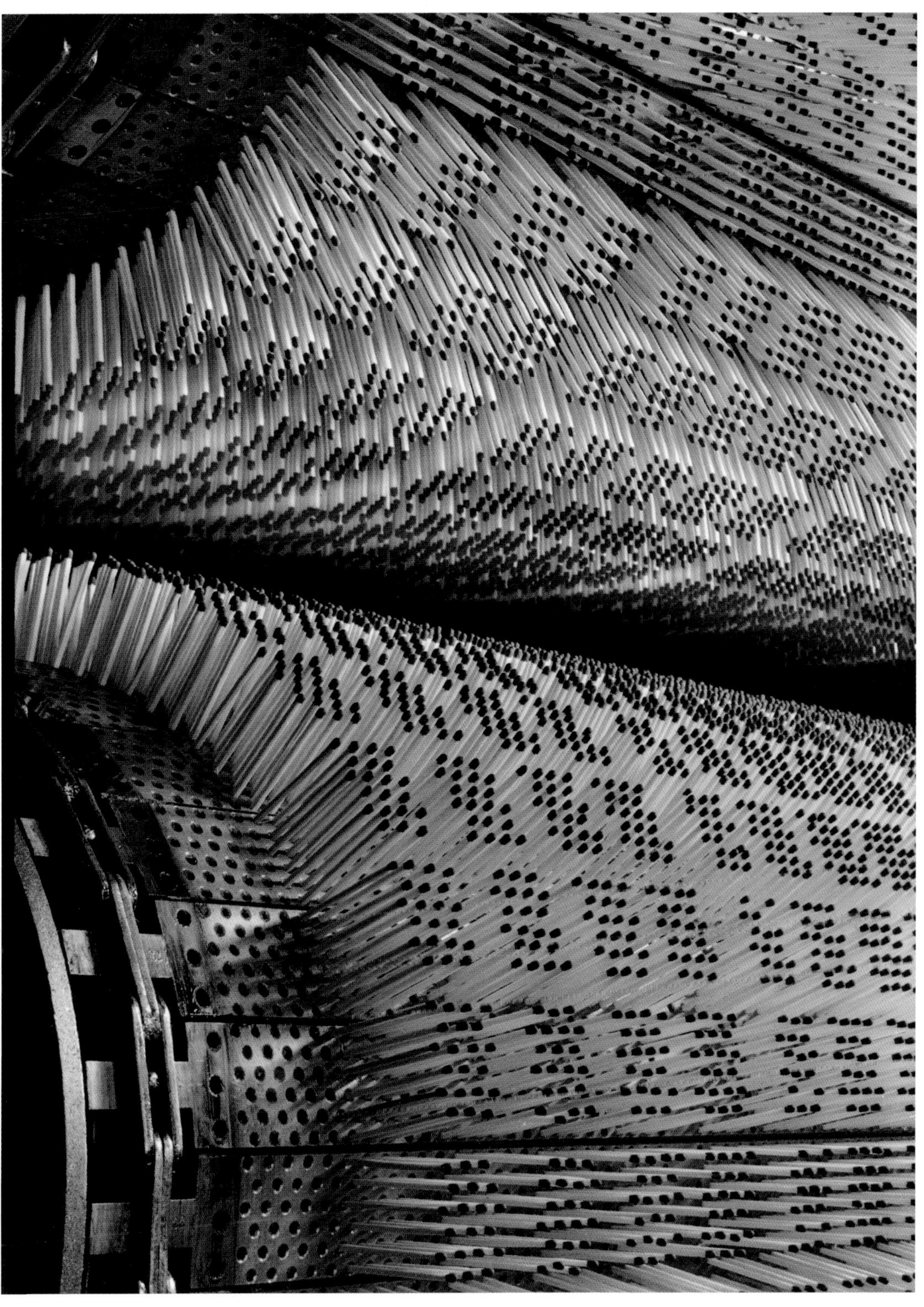

Manufacture of Matches at Bryant & May, Richmond, Victoria 1939
gelatin silver photograph; 51 × 36.3cm
nla.cat-vn3046458

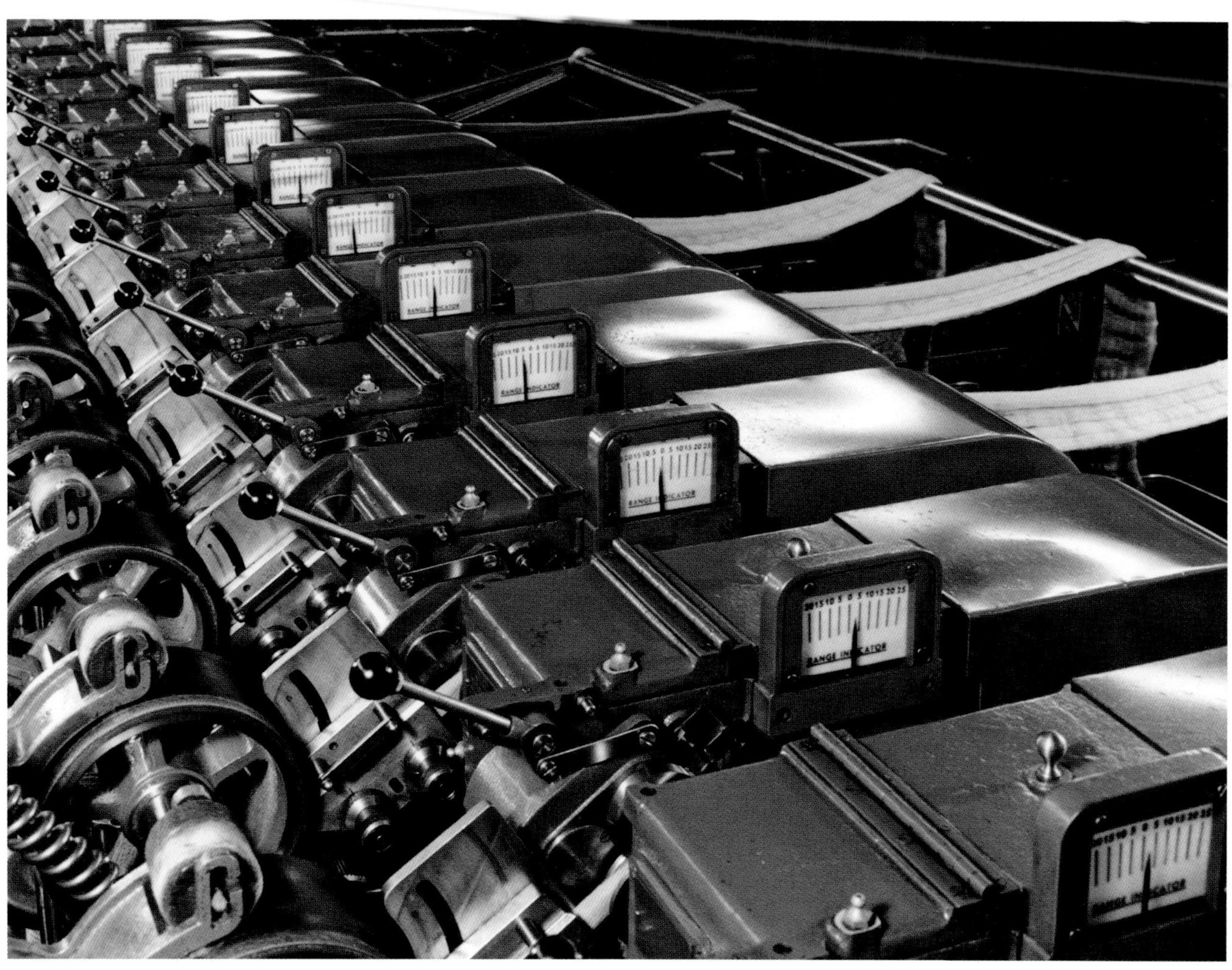

Machinery, Yarra Falls Limited, Abbotsford, Victoria 1960
gelatin silver photograph; 19.1 × 24.6cm
nla.cat-vn4398155

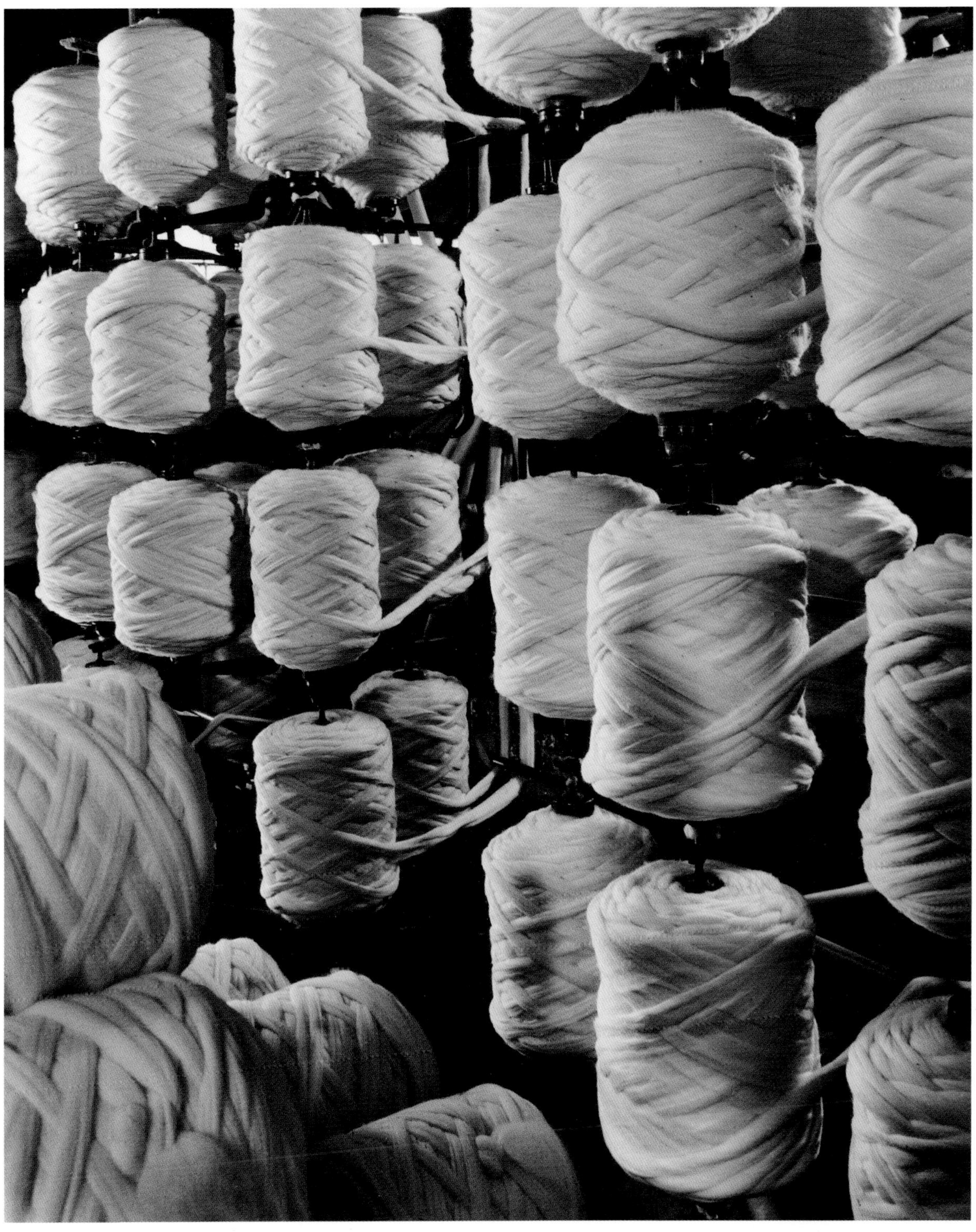

Wool Bobbins at Yarra Falls Limited, Abbotsford, Victoria 1960
gelatin silver photograph; 49.3 × 39.8cm
nla.cat-vn2235874

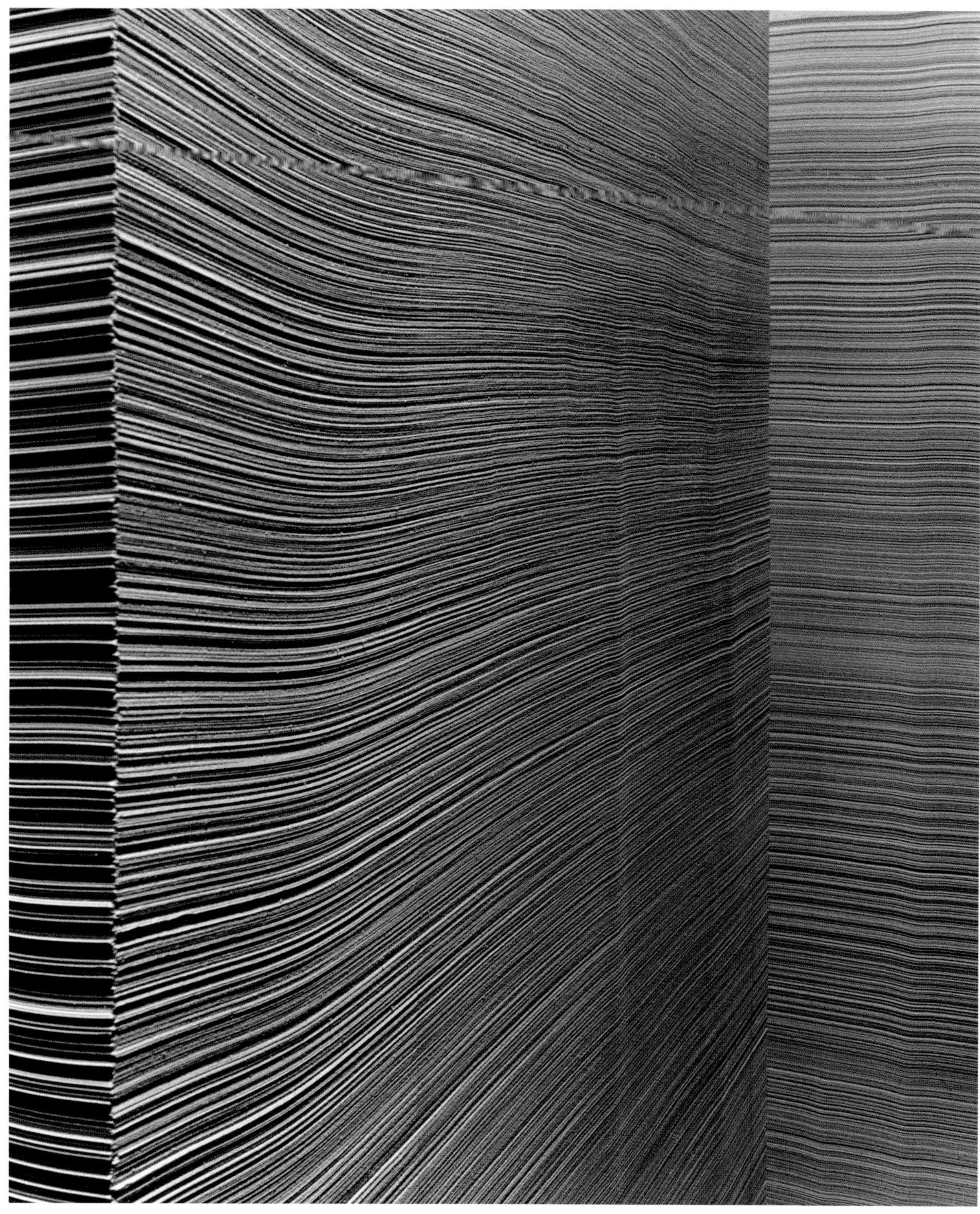

Associated Pulp and Paper Mills Fine Paper, Burnie, Tasmania 1962
gelatin silver photograph; 24.4 × 19.9cm
nla.cat-vn19777

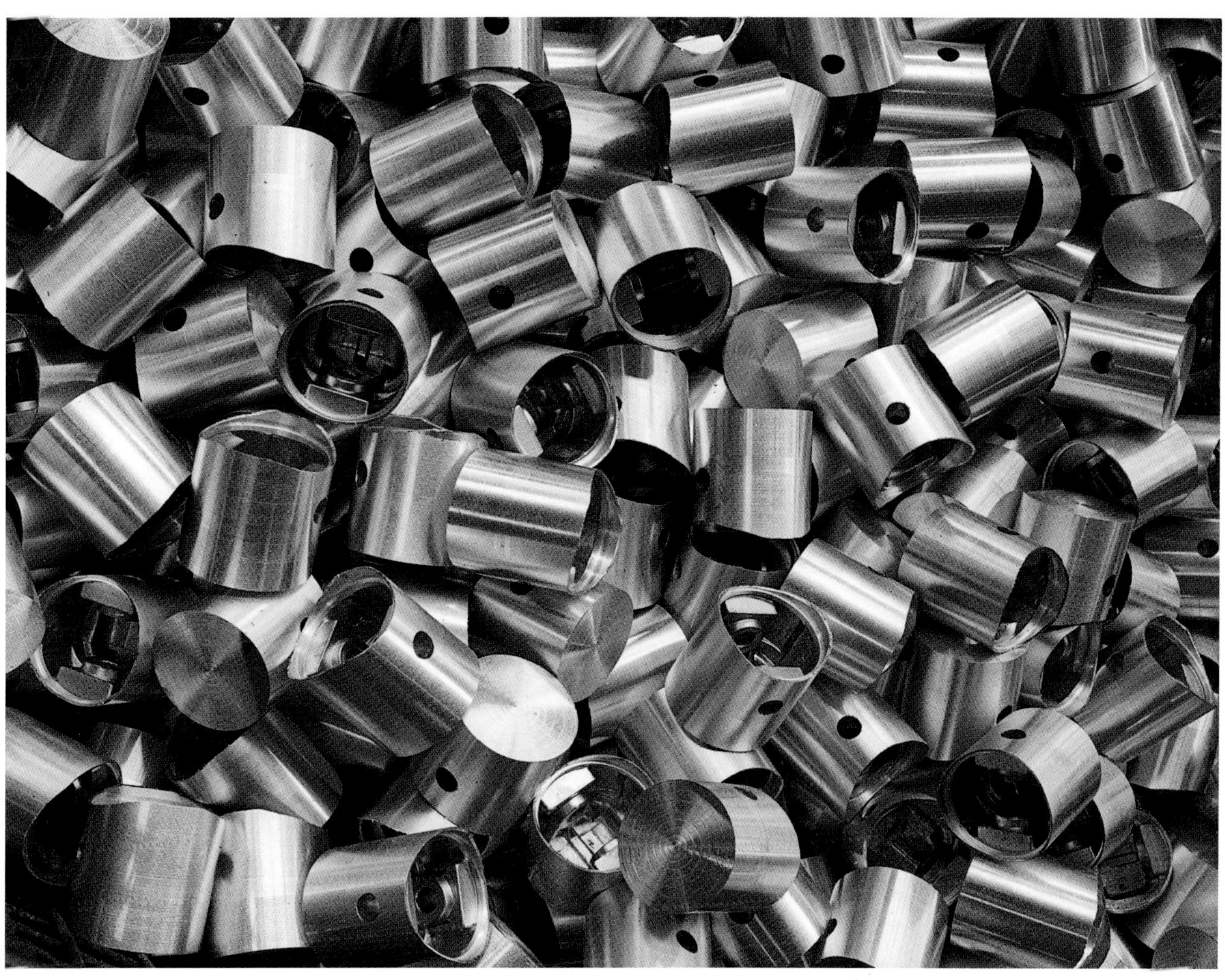

Comalco Aluminium Castings 1962
negative; 10 × 12.5cm
nla.cat-vn3291025

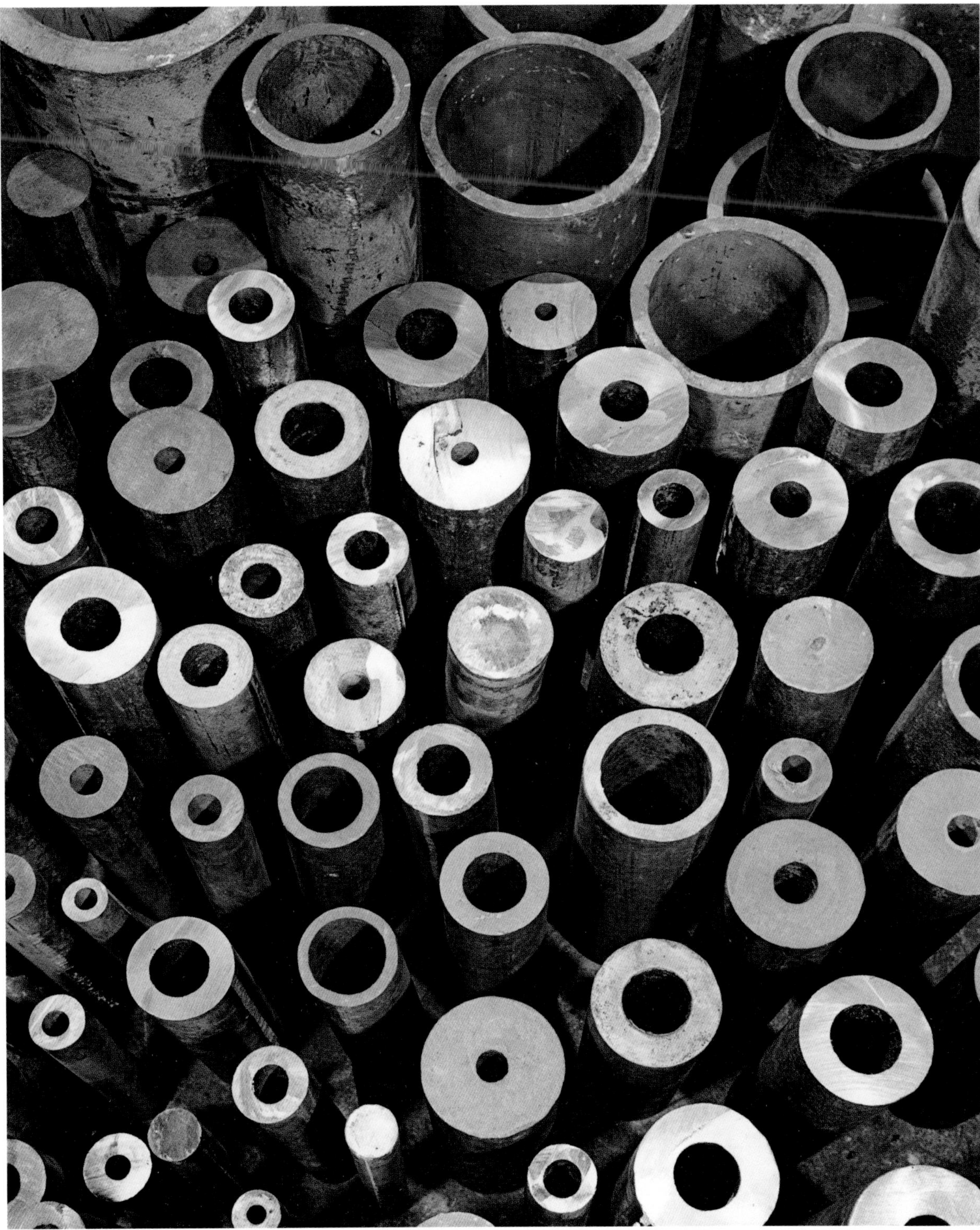

Bronze Pipes at the Adams Bronze Foundry, Melbourne, Victoria 1968
gelatin silver photograph; 24.1 × 19.2cm
nla.cat-vn1011670

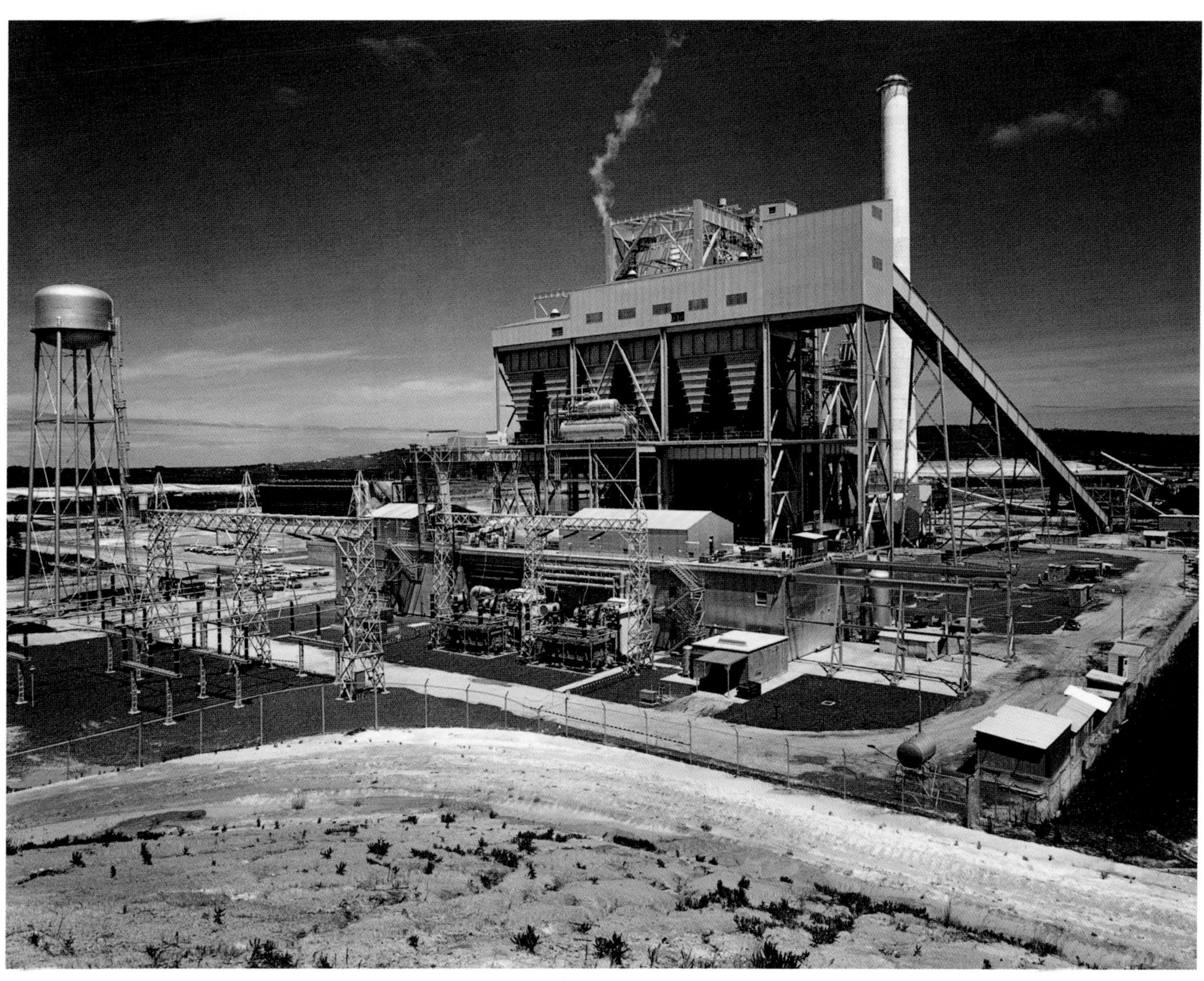

Power Station at Alcoa Coal Mine, Anglesea, Victoria 1969
gelatin silver photograph; 19.6 × 24.5cm
nla.cat-vn3943649

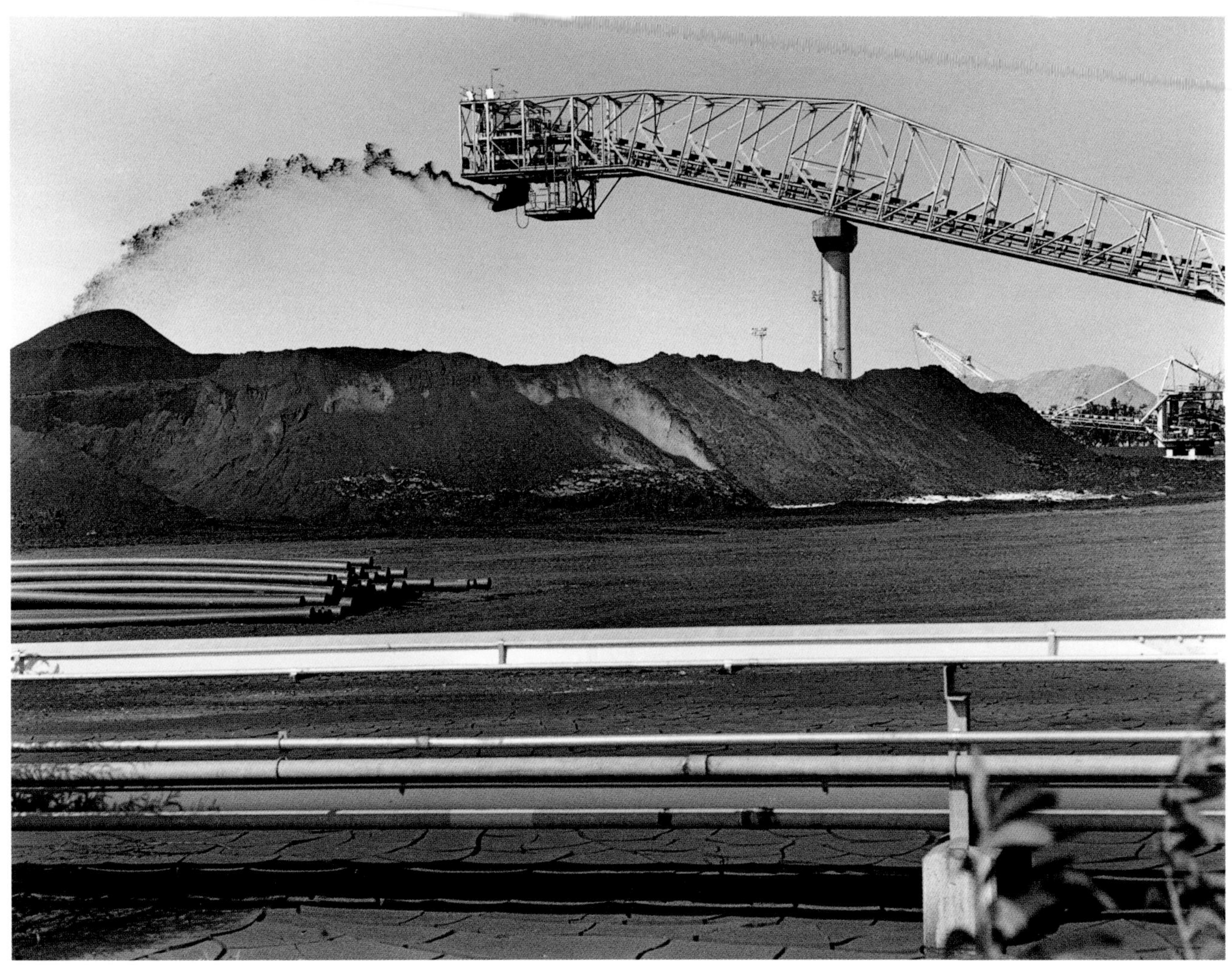

Stacker Reclaimer, German Creek Coal Mine, Queensland 1985
gelatin silver photograph; 19.4 × 24.6cm
nla.cat-vn1081515

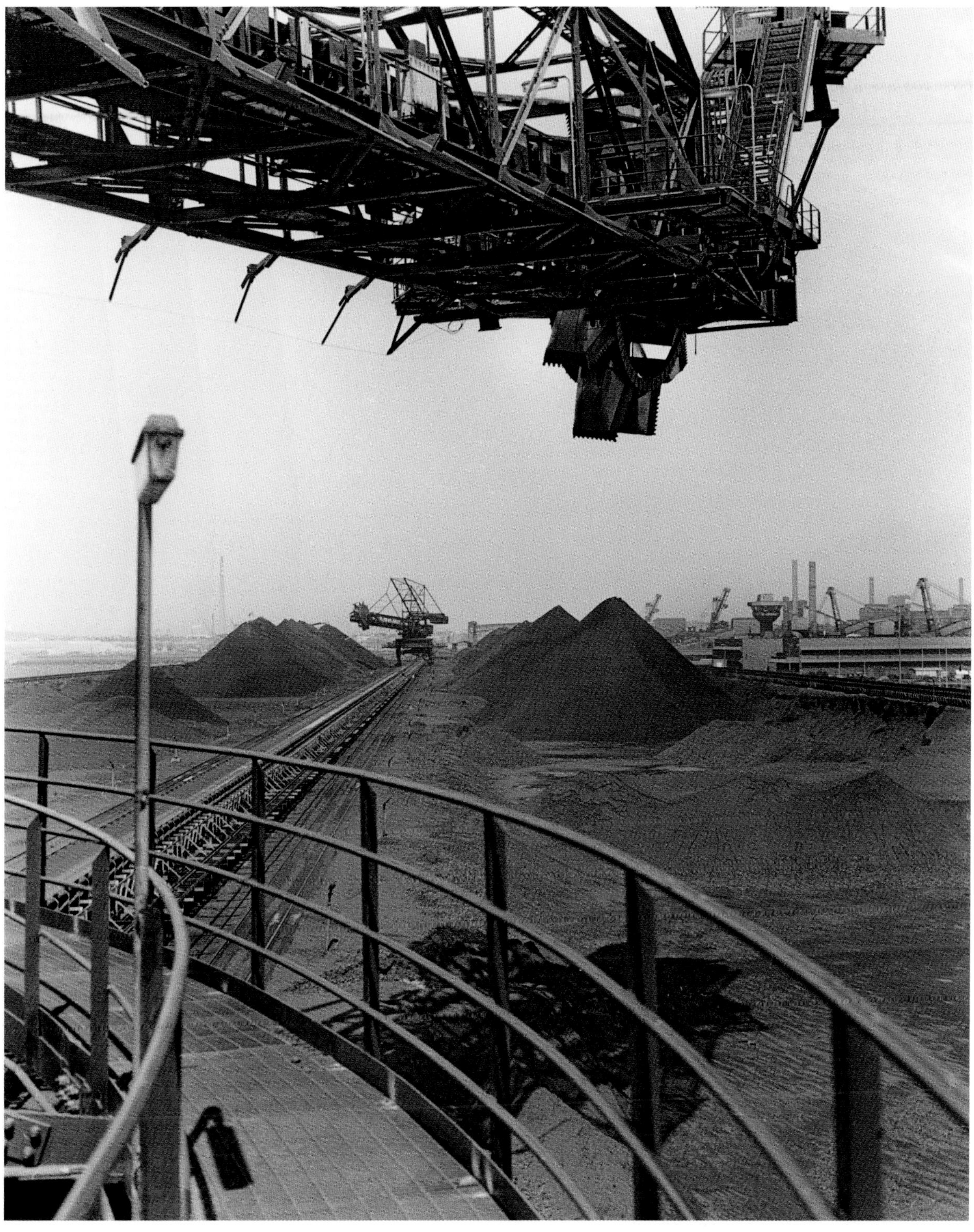

Stacker Reclaimer, Coal Terminal at Wollongong, New South Wales 1985
gelatin silver photograph; 24.5 × 19.6cm
nla.cat-vn2632033

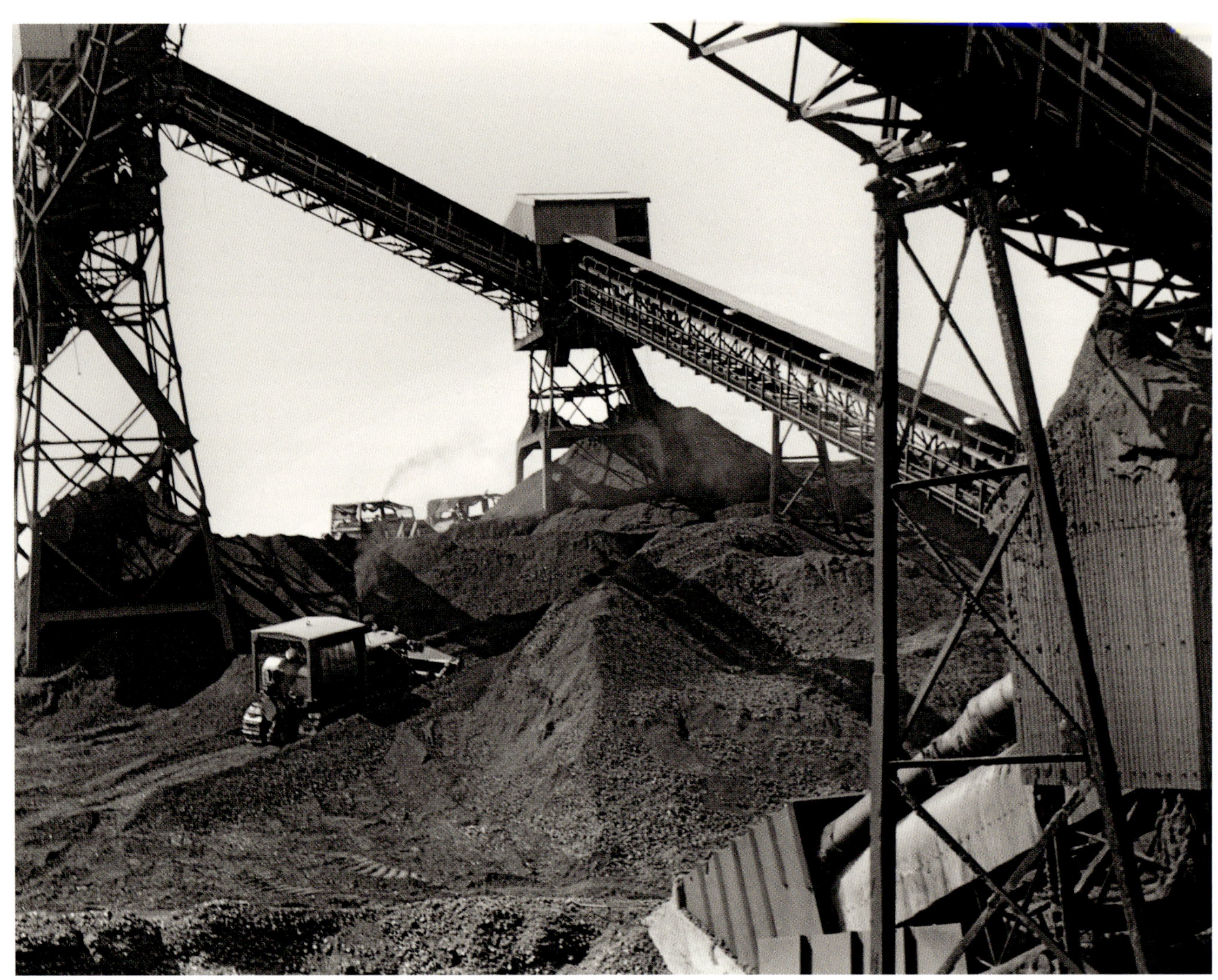

Stacking Coal, Belambi Coal Mine, New South Wales 1985
gelatin silver photograph; 19.5 × 24.3cm
nla.cat-vn1117177

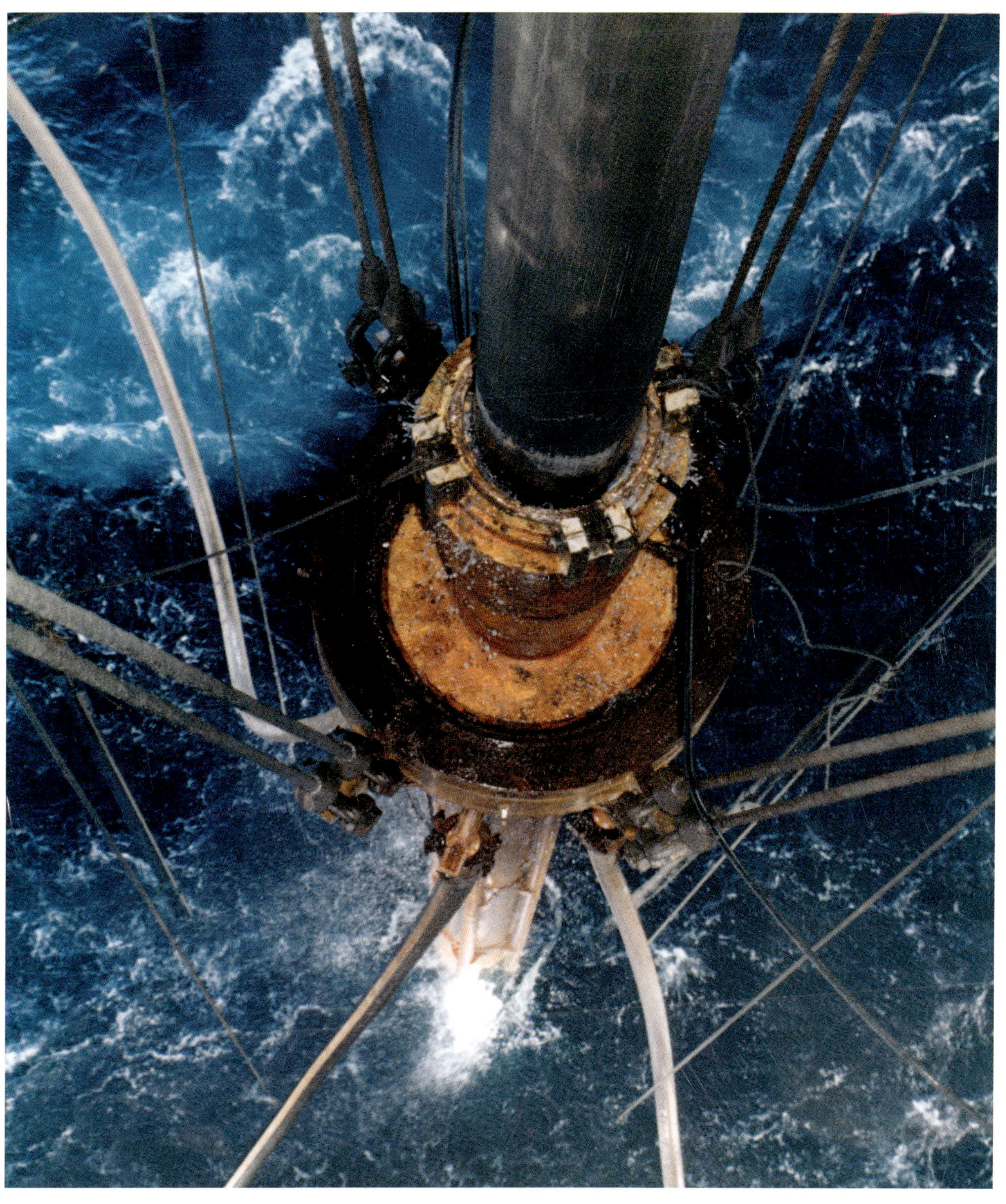

Drilling for Oil at Shell's 'Nymphea' Oil Rig in Bass Strait, Victoria 1983
type C photograph; 59.9 × 50.1cm
nla.cat-vn861662

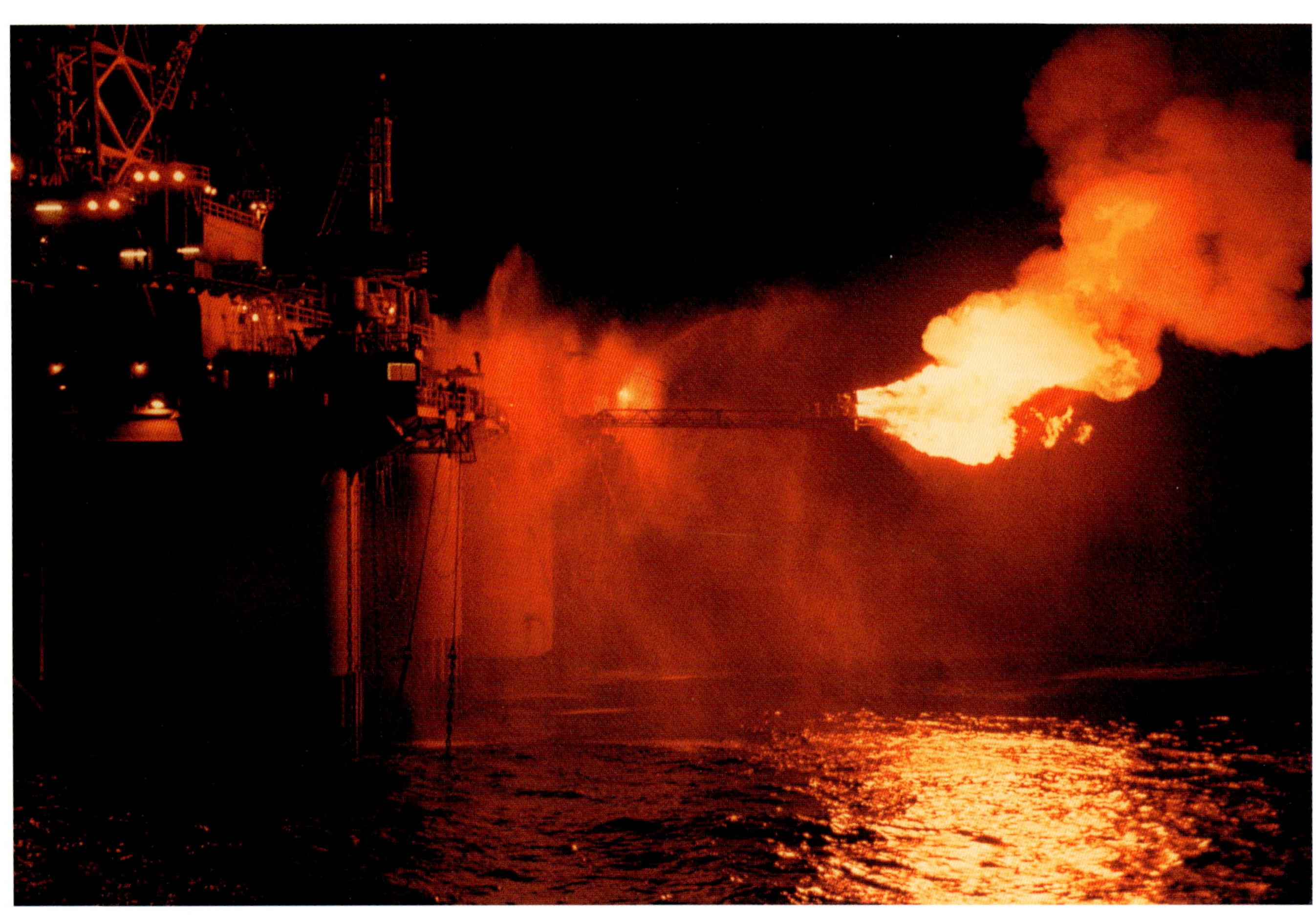

'Curtains of Fire', Shell's Drilling Rig, the 'Nymphea' in Bass Strait, Victoria 1983
type C photograph; 60.3 × 40.8cm
nla.cat-vn2494859